PUBLISHING
victorpublishing.co.uk

Also available...

AFTER THE LORD MAYOR'S SHOW

MILLWALL FOOTBALL CLUB

IN THE 1990s - Part One

MERV PAYNE

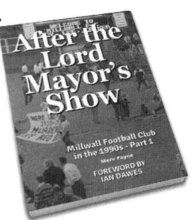

Starting the decade as a top flight club, Millwall were keen to regain that place after relegation at the end of the 89/90 season - and it would become increasingly important with the new world of riches that The Premier League would soon bring. Instead, their fans were taken on a 10-year roller coaster ride that included play-off drama, leaving their beloved Den, nearly going out of business and making a first trip to Wembley since World War Two, with plenty more in between. This is the story of Millwall's 1990s. It was life after the First Division, from the sublime to the ridiculous. Because we all know what comes after the Lord Mayor's Show...

PUBLISHING
victorpublishing.co.uk

SOUTH BERMONDSEY HOMESICK BLUES

MILLWALL FOOTBALL CLUB
IN THE 1990s
Part Two

Merv Payne

Acknowledgements

A big thank you to Alex Rae for providing the foreword for this book.

Massive thanks also to Dave Elson for the cover photography.

I'd also like to thank everyone who continues to support and encourage me - mostly via Twitter and Facebook - by buying these books, it is appreciated more than you know.

Contents

foreword

by ALEX RAE

SOUTH BERMONDSEY HOMESTEAD BLUES

Foreword

By Alex Rae

Like many Millwall footballers, Bob Pearson was instrumental in me signing for the club. Until then, my career had started at Celtic Boys Club which, as you can probably imagine is a bit unusual for a lifelong Glasgow Rangers fan - it went against everything I stood for, but they had a very good set up and a good track record for developing young footballers and gave me my first chance. I can't explain how excited I was at the age of fifteen and a half to be signed by Rangers though. One minute you're just a young a fan that's grown up watching Rangers, the next you're going into an environment with all the players I grew up adoring, guys like Derek Johnstone, Peter McCloy who won the 1972 European Cup Winners Cup and Davie Cooper who sadly passed away at just 40. It was surreal, one minute I'm out with my mates in the East End of Glasgow and the next I'm mingling with all these guys, but I have to be honest, I found the process difficult.

I realised straight away that it was a very dog-eat-dog environment. You hear about clubs trying to create a good set-up for players but what you don't realise is how much it's every man for himself at that level. You're constantly looking at the other apprentices and thinking: "What do I need to do to get a chance ahead of *him*?". There are so many other things going on, so many other ups and downs and things to deal with, not just the football, that are part of it, and it's hard.

About 18 months after I joined, Graeme Souness came in as manager and three months after that I was let go - although it was actually Walter Smith that did the firing as Graeme was busy sorting out the first team. I always remember the piece of advice that Walter gave me. He asked me: "How do you think you've done Alex?" to which I replied that I felt I'd done OK.

To my relief he replied: "So do we", but that was short-lived when he continued:

"We just don't think you're 100% committed. It doesn't matter what your job is, whether it's a footballer, a plumber, an electrician, whatever, you need to be 100% committed, so for that reason, we're letting you go."

At that point obviously I was devastated. If I'd been a boxer I'd have thrown the towel in, I was finished. I was seventeen and didn't know what the future held - like so many other young lads that have fallen through the game.

Then came something of a sliding door moment for me.

I got a call out of the blue at home one day from a man called Joe Woods. I didn't know how he'd got my number, but he asked me if I wanted to go and play semi-pro. It turned out that he got in touch with the lads released by the top Scottish clubs at the time - Rangers, Celtic, Hearts, Hibs, Aberdeen, Dundee United - and tried to help them get back into the game, so I started playing for a good standard club at that level called Bishopbriggs. Within four months of that, Falkirk, who were a second tier Scottish team then, came in for me and I did a three year apprenticeship there which was magnificent, and I'll tell you why: When you look at the game at development level these days, where under 18s and under 19s are playing tippy-tappy football, I was getting drop-volleyed by Falkirk's first team regulars for 100 games, and it provided me with the best possible education in the game. Falkirk were one of the stronger teams at that level and had some experienced players who had played in the top division and we managed to get promoted. I played some top flight football before we were relegated again. In that three years I had experienced promotion and relegation and really developed as a player.

In my last season we finished second and I scored a few goals and that's when the call came from Millwall.

It came at a good time for me because I was looking to get out of Glasgow where my lifestyle perhaps still wasn't quite conducive to professional football shall we say!

That's when I was reminded of Walter Smith's words. I always felt I was 100% committed in matches, but maybe not so much so in preparation and I felt a move would help this.

I was really excited about a move down to London, but perhaps a bit naive! I knew Millwall had just been relegated from the top division and had lots of well-known players and I thought I'd be leaving the modest surroundings of Falkirk's little Brockville ground (where it didn't take much of a shot to clear both the crossbar and the main stand!) for the glamorous world of London and a fancy stadium. On my first day, when I pulled up in Cold Blow Lane to the main entrance of The Den opposite a scrap yard I though: "What *is* this place!"

Then Bob Pearson took me in and I walked down the tunnel and looked out onto the pitch which looked lovely in the July sunshine and the first thing that struck me was the high fences all around the pitch and thought: "OOF!". I didn't really know that much about Millwall until after I arrived and heard about the Scottish dockers involved with the formation of the club and its Scottish affiliation, but

I certainly got a taste of the passion of the place when I made my home debut at The Den against Barnsley. We'd had a good result at Watford on the Saturday and I thought I'd done OK. During the Barnsley match I went over to take a quick throw-in in front of The Halfway Line and as I did, somebody poked me through the fence, then I heard: "OI, FACKIN' LIVEN UP!".

Fortunately though I got off to a good start, scored my first goal for the club that day and the fans were great with me. I don't think I took any more throw-ins though!

Ironically, as I arrived at the club, another midfielder went in the opposite direction. Terry Hurlock joined Rangers and I was gutted because my brief experience with him was certainly memorable.

We were at a training camp at Aberystwyth, it was pretty brutal with sand dune runs and every day ended with a five mile run along the beach. It was my first day and I was keen to make a good impression and after coming fifth I was happy with my performance but was keen to get into the top three or four. By the end of the week we were on the final one of these murder runs and, coming up to the finish mark I was well placed and put a bit of a spurt on.

Suddenly I can hear this voice: "GO ON SON, GO ON!"

I looked up and it was Hurlock, he'd suddenly appeared from nowhere in front of me, his trademark permed hair was soaking wet with what I thought was sweat from his run.

That evening we're sat having our meal and I plucked up the courage to speak to him (bearing in mind I'd only just joined the club and he didn't know me from Adam) so I asked how he managed to finish in front of me from nowhere.

"You know how I did it son?" he explained. "I took a pound coin out with me."

I was even more puzzled by now, "How did that help?" I asked.

"I nipped out of the sand dunes and used the pound coin to jump on a bus, which dropped me off half a mile from the finish. Then, when I saw all you silly c***s coming, I dipped my 'ead in the water and ran the last half mile."

I thought: this fella is magnificent, it's a shame I never got to play alongside him! He reminds me of my Dad. Every time I see him in the years since we stopped playing he'll give me a big bear hug, a dig in the ribs and say: "Alright ya little fucker!"

My first season was good, but ended in disappointment with the play-off defeat against Brighton but I loved playing under Bruce Rioch because he was a strong disciplinarian and I needed that at the time. When Mick McCarthy took over I must admit I found it hard to accept the transition from Mick the fellow player to Mick the Gaffer. He wanted to switch me from central midfield to right midfield which I wasn't happy with - and he stuck me on the bench. I was there for about six or seven games then one day he tells me he wants me to play: in right midfield. So I played, in right midfield, and scored two goals which made me realise if the gaffer wants to play you in right midfield, right back or even in goal I'll play - another lesson learned!

Mick never sugar-coated anything, he said it like it was which I really appreciate as a player, a lot of players do and it's no surprise that he's still managing now 30 years later.

Obviously one thing that's always stayed with me is the atmosphere that the Millwall fans could generate - both at the old Den and new one. It was a bit strange at first when we moved but we had a couple of big cup games there and the noise they made was unbelievable. Obviously I would love to have got to the Premier League with Millwall, and I would still love to see them there - can you imagine the noise they would make at those stadiums - and The Den? In what would turn out to be my final season at Millwall I watched the likes of Fuchs, Malkin and the Russians come in on much better contracts than me and it was quite frustrating. It all boiled over before the crucial last three games when I got sent off for a bit of fisticuffs with Oldham's Chris Makin and I ended up watching our last match at Ipswich with the Millwall fans as we were relegated on the final day. As hard as it was for me then, I knew it was time to leave.

I did get offered the chance to come back in 2006 when Ray Wilkins invited me back for a couple of seasons but I had just left Rangers, my family was settled north of the border and I didn't think I could manage the travelling up and down the motorway after doing it for fourteen years. Besides which, I didn't want to let the Millwall fans down by not being able to produce my best form.

I was lucky to enjoy some Premier League football with Sunderland and Wolves and eventually realised my dream of not only playing but scoring for Glasgow Rangers. My playing career had gone full circle having been rejected by Walter Smith at Ibrox all those years ago. Making the breakthrough at Millwall will always be a special time for me - especially the noise of those fans, those FA Cup runs and playing alongside some great players like Sheringham who is the best player I've played with.

Millwall is a brilliant club which will always have a special place in my heart and I still look out for their results now. I really enjoyed playing in front of the Millwall fans and I'd like to think that I always played with passion and gave it my all and that those fans appreciated that. Hopefully they'll get to see The Lions in the Premier League one day soon.

South Bermondsey homesick blues

Introduction

The Premier League was just three years old but was already working its magic. For some it was every bit the wonderful, bright and sparkling new dawn that they felt football needed. The Beautiful Game now had a rightful place of dominance in popular culture. The swagger and glamour that was evident only on occasions through the much scoffed-at 1970s playboy pastiches of George Best in the 60s was no longer mocked. They were worshipped. Where once the non-footballing public looking from the outside rolled their eyes at the Frank Worthingtons and Malcolm Allisons of a sport that dared to transcend its working class roots, football was now upwardly mobile and everyone was taking notice.

Rather than: "Oh look at them, aren't they embarrassing...", it was now a case of: "Wow, look at them, aren't they amazing..." and: "I want to *be* them".

The start of a football season was no longer just excitedly counted down by giddy schoolboys. A television campaign heralding the latest season was trailed with all the glitter and glam and family inclusiveness of Christmas.

So it began. Football reinvented itself. But how did we get here? A decade after it was a global pariah, viewed as nothing more than a ghastly enabler for drunken yobs to travel the country and Europe fighting, smashing, even killing anything in its path. Played out in dreary, grey crumbling death-traps of arenas where yet more people perished due to the neglected archaic state of its facilities.

Back in the summer of 1985, to admit you were a football fan was akin to confessing your human failings as an addict. You were in a minority. You were part of an almost exclusively working class male subculture that few people outside of the sport could comprehend. Those glitz and glamour days of the 1970s had long gone. Those innocent times when Dad took his son to the match had been spoiled by the spectre of hooliganism it seemed. Even television turned its back on the game for a while as English football began a sentence for a list of crimes too long and sickening to contemplate. To visit a football ground in the 1985-86 season would seemingly make you complicit to the Luton riots where Millwall fans brought the FA Cup quarter final to a halt, the carnage at Stamford Bridge when Chelsea played Sunderland in a League Cup semi final and thugs confronted police on horseback on the pitch, the death of a young fan when Birmingham fans clashed with rival supporters from Leeds and a wall collapsed in the chaos. This particular incident on the same day that life was lost on an horrendous scale not seen in the UK since the Ibrox disaster in 1971 as 56 fans perished in a fire as the antiquated wooden stand at Bradford's Valley Parade was engulfed in fire.

Football was it seemed embarking on an orgy of self-harm that would surely lead to its ultimate demise and it all came to an astonishing climax at the very highest level of the sport, involving the name that for so long had been synonymous with all that was good in the game: Liverpool.

The Heysel Stadium riot during the 1985 European Cup Final between Liverpool and Juventus showed a global audience that football was rotten, it was finished, and the blame lay squarely at the feet of one country: England.

Banished from Europe, football in England looked to be ready to be consigned to the scrap heap. It hobbled through the rest of the decade where mercifully the hooliganism abated both at home - and thanks to a ban on all clubs taking part in European competition - abroad. A tougher stance was taken against any forms of unrest and the game was forced to accept it had not looked after its paying customers for decades and was now paying the price. Even when things started to feel as though they were improving towards the end of the eighties, tragedy struck once more to underline just how critically the game was getting it wrong. The huge fences erected to stop one of football's ills exacerbated another as once again innocent fans perished after simply going to the match. Hillsborough was a stark reminder that football had to change from top to bottom. It needed not just a few coins tossed at it from the terrestrial television pot to fund one or two marquee signings. It needed a rebirth, a rebrand, to have mass appeal in order to draw in the crowds not just in the stands on a Saturday or Sunday afternoon but from their armchairs on nights of the week when watching football was previously unheard of.

As the nineties began, a previously unheard of television channel, known only perhaps to those privileged few lucky enough to have 'cable TV' in their area emerged.

With English clubs finally being allowed back into European competition, it was felt that their exile would have pushed them down the pecking order which would cause the game at the highest level almost as much harm as the ban itself. The struggle to regain the supremacy it had enjoyed in the late seventies and early eighties when no other country could get their hands on European club football's top prize could only be strengthened quickly by a turbo-charged injection of cash. This was one of the first justifications for forming the FA Premier League when talks began in 1991. From there things moved quickly and by 1992 the top flight clubs resigned from the Football League and the Premier League began as a limited company with exclusive live saturation coverage on Sky Sports.

This, the games cynics decried, was the beginning of the end for football as we knew it. Now the fairytales of smaller less glamorous clubs climbing from the lower leagues to compete in the top flight (as Millwall had done in 1988) would now surely be consigned to the game's folklore.

The fact that Wimbledon were one of the founder members and a recipient of the unprecedented investment didn't really cut it. They were the nouveau riche, doomed to be seen as traitors of their lower league roots but never accepted by their lofty neighbours.

With Manchester United winning the first two Premier League titles - and making that a league and FA Cup double in 1994 - the unstoppable bandwagon had begun and it seemed, despite the best efforts of the likes of Norwich and Aston Villa (who of course had won the league title back in 1981) none of the less-fashionable names it seemed would get a look in. That was, of course, exactly how the top clubs - and the Premier League wanted it.

But football always finds a way.

In 1995 Blackburn Rovers shocked two-time title winners United by wrestling their crown from them. Let's be honest though, this was no humble tale of how an unfancied outsider had come from nowhere to shock the wealthy establishment by taking the honours on nothing more than a wing and a prayer and shoestring budget with a squad of unlikely lads.

Blackburn's wealthy owner Jack Walker had decided to short-circuit the system. Ploughing millions of his personal fortune into team investment that even United couldn't compete with, he'd secured the services of the best players in the game and, it would be fair to argue that, even before the giants of Old Trafford, who already had in place a talented, mostly home-grown squad, had become the first club of the modern era to buy success.

This was a clarion call to every club outside the top flight. Like a modern day gold rush, football club chairmen and directors from clubs right across England in all three of the Football League's divisions started to realise that you really did have to speculate to accumulate. You had to gamble. Investment was sought, loans were taken out, every sofa at every club boardroom was pillaged for its hidden coinage. Football was going to sell its shirt and risk ruin if it had to in order to reach this promised land. Footballing glory and riches were not unattainable as was once feared when the Premier League began, they just cost a little bit more. With a bit of investment, wheeling and dealing and calculated risk, it was possible to stake your claim in the Premier League's land of milk and honey. Forget simply existing. Forget nurturing youth, complex scouting networks and the time-consuming practice of waiting for local talent to blossom while you trod water in mid-table obscurity. Now was the time to spend, spend, spend and aim high. I mean, come on, what have you got to lose?

SO[]th Be[]mo[]d[]se[] ho[]me[][] B[]e[]

95/96

oh those
russians....

SOUth BermonDsey homesick Blues

1

JUST LIKE STARTING OVER

It was a new dawn in SE16 in every sense. A new team had been assembled which at first glance appeared, in both experience and ability, to be head and shoulders above what the rest of what Division One had to offer. There was also a distinct feeling of a new culture at The Den. For the first time Millwall were seen as *genuine* contenders. Not plucky outsiders in with a chance, not even the antici-pated success of 1990 when they had just been relegated from the top flight and battled - ultimately unsuccessfully - to regain that place at the first attempt with one of their strongest ever squads.

Even in 1990, playing their home games at their legendary old Den made them always the underdog. Of course Millwall fans liked it that way and most hated the wrench of leaving the old place in 1993. But, as that scar began to heal, many accepted the fact that, if they wanted that precious place in the top division back, sacrifices had to be made.

Some of those sacrifices seemed harsh. The sales of Chris Armstrong, Jon Goodman, Kenny Cunningham and Colin Cooper seemed to undermine the very purpose of getting back to the top. However, investment during the summer of

1995 convinced them that, whilst they may have appeared to have taken one or two steps backwards in recent seasons, the transfer dealings that Mick McCarthy was able to carry out could only be seen as several huge strides forward.

There was a feeling around the sun-drenched Den in July and August 1995 that could only be compared to the summer of 1987. Almost every week it seemed The South London Press was announcing another impressive signing.

"Herr We Go!" trumpeted the SLP as Uwe Fuchs joined Chris Malkin in Millwall's reportedly £1.1 million double coup. A strike pairing that had found goals in Division One easy to come by. That was half the battle surely? A defence overseen by a manager in McCarthy who had proved one of the best in the business on a worldwide scale was also reason to believe that, rather than the seat-of-their-pants roller coaster, will they won't they journey to success back in 1988, this would surely be a season long lap of honour to the title.

If Lions fans needed anything else to whet their appetites, the winners of the Football League's now top division of course lifted the original Football League championship trophy - the very same iconic silverware that the all-conquering Liverpool teams had raised in their dominant late 70s and 80s era - and so many famous names before them.

Everything it seemed was perfect. The new stadium, whilst still a little awkward, was grudgingly starting to feel like home, the spectre of sanctions following the Derby trouble in the play-off defeat of 1994 were now consigned to history. So however, was the man who had presided over them so gallantly, fighting Millwall's corner, as he had done so steadfastly as the club's Chairman for nine years: Reg Burr.

It had been announced at the end of the previous season

that Burr was to step down as Chairman and be replaced by board member and lifelong Lions fan Peter Mead.

Burr had first become involved in the club back in 1974 where he was a board member until the Alan Thorne regime took over. He left in 1982 but returned in a blaze of glory as part of the consortium that saved the club from financial ruin in 1986.

Ravaged by debt and a lengthy repair bill to The Den to meet the new safety requirements in the wake of the Bradford disaster, Burr took the helm as chairman and installed Mead as his right hand man.

Difficult decisions were always the order of the day from the moment he took the position and one of these was to entrust John Docherty as manager to replace the departing George Graham. It was to prove one of many moves that initially made Burr an unpopular figure, but he was never one to shy away, shift the blame or play politics with fans. He believed in telling it as it was - as much as you could in the cauldron of football administration. One of his first appearances to Millwall supporters was in what became an iconic pose, slumped forebodingly over one of The Den's yellow crush barriers, mandatory cigar in hand, looking for all the world like the ghost of Millwall future warning of bad times to come if things didn't change. At the same time promising to move heaven and earth to bring the happy times back to The Den, just as long as the fans kept their faith in him.

They did, after a fashion, through what was a difficult 1986/87 season that could easily have seen the club relegated once more to the third tier of English football and into the same oblivion that it had been thrown amongst with demotion in 1979. They survived, just, and Burr then set about an unprecedented investment programme that resulted in promotion to the top flight for the first time in the club's 103 year history. Both Burr and Docherty were hailed as club heroes. Once again, never one to fear change, Burr pushed on with more unpopular moves - the most controversial being that which took the club away from The Den. Many chairmen before Burr had talked the talk, of Superdens and new developments, but Burr was the only one to walk the walk.

He now struck a new pose and whilst never one to wear a sunshine smile, looked altogether happier - still with cigar in hand - against the backdrop of Millwall's impressive new stadium. Like a well-meaning parent, Burr knew what was best but never forgot the importance of the fans at Millwall.

He always fought the fans corner, even when he appeared to be waging a battle he couldn't possibly win. His now famous quote will echo around the Internet message forums and social media platforms as the latest pile-on sees all quarters condemn Millwall's supporters in the wake of yet another media feeding frenzy:

"Millwall Football Club is a convenient coat peg upon which football and society can hang its ills"

While that is the sentence most quoted for Reg Burr, it should not be the quote that defined him and his time at the club. A measure of his respect and understanding of Millwall Football Club and the fans was never better illustrated than this quote taken from an interview in 1988:

"I will not condemn our people, I am not frightened of them, and I am not ashamed of them. Noone will ever make me say our supporters are scum. Never."

Reg Burr's nine years as Millwall Chairman was, by football club chairman standards, a great success. If there are any notes of sadness or regret they are probably that he never got to realise the dream that he truly believed he could achieve of establishing Millwall in the top flight for the long term. Hamstrung by the club's limited finances at an out-of-date stadium, the move was, he felt, necessary to take one last shot at that dream. Sadly, in his tenure, it wasn't to be and the other factor that many will point out perhaps prevented that dream from being realised - violence - which undoubtedly held the club back in terms of investment - will never have been blamed by Burr, such was his respect for Millwall supporters.

It was also a shame that, as with many fans, the natural reaction to a club chairman is animosity and mistrust. Many will not have taken the time to read Burr's programme notes, skimming past them assuming it was just more bullshit toeing the club line and telling them to behave. That couldn't have been further from the truth and very few in his position would have had the guts to constantly put their head above the parapet.

The banner that trailed across the Den pitch after the final game at the ground against Bristol Rovers announcing "HERE LIES THE DEN 1910-1993 MURDERED BY REG BURR" would have infuriated most chairmen in Burr's position who had moved heaven and earth to secure the long term future of the club with a move to a new stadium. Burr found it hilarious.

Millwall fans have always admired strength, whether it be in a Harry Cripps or Terry Hurlock tackle, or in the vocal power that belies their number on the terraces. It is hoped that Millwall fans also recognised and respected the strength of character that was Reg Burr.

He said his official farewell in typical fashion in the programme for the final match of the previous season:

"There is never an ideal time to say goodbye — particularly to this club which has been my sole preoccupation for so many years. I look back over the last nine years with pride. Together we have come a long, long way and enjoyed

a level of success which exceeds the expectations we had when we started out with less than nine outfield players that John Doc wanted to play. Inevitably we have had bad days but on balance we have arguably had the best nine years in the club's history. Certainly, like all large families, we have had our differences from time to time when I have been forced to make hard decisions, but I would like to think that you did and do know, that all I have ever wanted was success for Millwall. I feel happy in the thought that the club now has a brilliant group of young players and that the sub-structure of the playing side is probably in better shape than it has ever been, with a number of exciting young players whose presence should ensure a bright future. We all have to be proud of the stadium which gives the club the opportunity to have top class football at the New Den for many years to come. I know you sing "No one likes us — we don't care" but I truly do like you and do care, even when you made me angry. I have enjoyed my nine years as your Chairman — I would not have missed it for anything. Thank you for giving me the opportunity. I am sure you will give Peter Mead your full support for the future success of Millwall. I wish you well."

It was a typically candid and informal sign-off and you could only hope that, as fans arrived for the first game of the new season, they were aware that Reg Burr had left the building and how much gratitude they owed him for his hard work. Now it was time to move on. A new start, a new chairman, a new team in what was still a new stadium. It was time for a new future. It was just like starting over.

2

SLOW and steady...

June 1995
Liverpool pay a British record £8.5 million
for Nottingham Forest striker Stan Collymore;
Norwich City agree compensation with Wycombe
Wanderers for new manager Martin O'Neil; Arsenal
Manager Bruce Rioch makes Inter Milan's Dennis
Bergkamp his first signing, paying £7.5 million
for the Dutch star; Tottenham pay £4.5 million for
Crystal Palace's former Millwall striker Chris
Armstrong.
July 1995
Former Arsenal and Millwall manager George
Graham is found guilty of taking illegal payments
in respect of transfers; Teenage girls across the
country are placed on suicide watch after Robbie
Williams leaves Take That; Five people including
former Millwall striker John Fashanu are accused
of match fixing.
August 1995
John Fashanu announces retirement from the game
due to injury; Pubs in England are permitted to
remain open throughout Sunday afternoon for the
first time; Unemployment is now at 2,315,300 – one
of the lowest figures recorded in the last four
years; The English Football League season starts
on Saturday August 12th...

Peter Mead's heart must have sunk a little when he saw the sparsely populated Den stands for the season's opener. With the greatest respect, Grimsby were never a hot ticket in any circumstances, and I'm sure the fans of The Mariners who had made the long trip down from the home of the Findus Crispy Pancake will have been equally uninspired by a first day trip to The Den. The usual caveats prevailed of course. Many were on holiday for the August 12th curtain-raiser and certain level of time-ingrained cynicism of Millwall's many false dawns would have meant that many will have chosen to wait for proof of The Lions' actual promotion credentials before setting foot inside The Den.

Many had been here before, the Peter Anderson reign being the most bitter of experiences, when unprecedented investment brought not unrivalled success, but unmitigated disaster.

While it may have been viewed, in terms of opposition, attendance and even starting line-up as something of a false start (new striker Uwe Fuchs was serving a suspension held over from his Middlesbrough loan the previous season) those that decided to put their faith in this brave new beginning were rewarded by a promising start.

The starting line-up of Keller, Bennett, Thatcher, Doyle, Witter, Stevens, Savage, Rae, Dixon, Malkin and Van Blerk omitted no less than three of those summer signings and was perhaps a sensible move by McCarthy to bed in his new look squad and get the season going with a steady progression and many of the players that had served so well in the previous season's unremarkable campaign.

With less than ten minutes on the clock, Alex Rae, one of the stalwarts of the club and a player who would surely be a vital part in the master plan, gratefully stroked home a penalty to give The Lions a ninth-minute lead. With just over half an hour gone Chris Malkin made it two. His debut goal greeted by as much a sign of relief as joy. Here was a player who had regularly scored goals at this level for Tranmere but so often such moves from north to south turn sour. Getting a goal so soon into his career in the capital was surely a good sign.

The floodgates did not open. Had they done, it may have provided some false over-optimism that this was going to be one of many easy wins on the way to the title. Grimsby's consolation goal on the hour didn't trouble Millwall's lead and a thoroughly satisfactory, if totally unspectacular match ended 2-1. The first of 46 hurdles had been negotiated with what could be argued as not McCarthy's full strength team. There was an encouraging blend of youth and experience. One such bright point of the former was Ben Thatcher.

The home grown left back was one of the few players left at the club who had come through the ranks and looked better with every game under his belt. At the opposite end of the spectrum was Kerry Dixon. The legendary, record-breaking Chelsea striker was coming to the Autumn of his career and slotting in nicely in the absence of Fuchs. Savage and Van Blerk continued to prove their value as industrious and creative members of The Lions' midfield, belying their humble origins from where they arrived to stake long-term places in the Millwall starting line-up.

Witter and Stevens formed an obvious steadfast alliance in the centre of defence and Keller was the consummate safe pair of hands. If Micky Bennett and Maurice Doyle were seen as wildcard entries into this developing Premier League-elect side, they were doing a steady job of it.

In fact 'steady' would be the best way to describe every-thing at The Den as fans left the stadium that afternoon. Steady was good. It wasn't a 4-0 home defeat, a drab goalless draw or a tumultuous victory that could never be bettered in the next game. It was steady, and we all know that slow and steady wins the race.

It was the next match that veteran striker Dixon really showed his value. At Vale Park, where Millwall had rarely enjoyed success, the match appeared to be petering out into a goalless draw with both sides cancelling each other out. Port Vale's regular season-long mission of survival was carved out of such bore draws, but Dixon had other ideas. Just after the hour mark, with Millwall doggedly knocking on the door for a breakthrough, Dixon showed all of his years of guile and experience as a grabber of goals from nothing situations by swivelling in a crowded penalty area to fire into the top corner of the home side's net to give The Lions the lead.

Now it was the turn of the defence to do their job and thirty minutes of resistance was barely enough to break sweat on the brow of Tony Witter who lapped up the adulation of the travelling Lions fans after the final whistle. Together with Stevens, the pair looked unbeatable and whilst some might have seen it as another hard-earned win against a side destined for a season of struggle, these are the wins on which promotions are won. So many times in the past Millwall sides had found their best form in matches against the top sides only to come unstuck against the league's strugglers. Here they had perhaps proved that weakness had been eradicated from their game and, with it, an inability to collect vital points on the road had maybe also been improved upon.

With winless Southend next to visit The Den, things were already starting to go according to plan. Only a fool pays any attention to the league tables after two matches obviously, but a good start was nevertheless essential for Millwall to instil confidence not only in its players but much more importantly the fans.

Endsleigh League Division One - August 26th 1995						
	P	W	D	L	F	A	PTS
1. MILLWALL	2	2	0	0	3	1	6
2. Tranmere	2	1	1	0	4	2	4
3. Reading	2	1	1	0	4	3	4
4. Stoke City	2	1	1	0	4	3	4
5. Norwich City	2	1	1	0	3	1	4

The encouraging start buoyed the attendance at The Den for the visit of Southend by over two thousand more than the 8,500 that had witnessed the win against Grimsby a fortnight before but, in typical circumstances, as soon as the weight of expectation had come into play, coupled with the assumption that the early strugglers from the Essex coast would provide easy picking for a third consecutive win, disappointment wasn't far behind.

With Fuchs now available for selection but his replacement Dixon making it impossible for McCarthy to drop him after his match-winning goal at Port Vale, the German forward started on the bench and was brought on for Dixon with 20 minutes remaining of a game where Millwall had tried unsuccessfully to breach a stubborn Shrimpers' back line. Stalemate at home may have robbed Millwall of its meaningless top of the table position, but it was by no means a spanner in the works. It was the trip to fellow early promotion hopefuls Reading where the spanners came out.

The Lions' midweek trip to Elm Park got off to the worst possible start when Reading player-boss Mick Gooding scored a spectacular opener from 30 yards to give the hosts the lead going into half time.

New signing Malkin was looking worryingly out of sorts and ex-Reading man Dixon was kept quiet as McCarthy decided to make a change and bring on Fuchs at the start of the second half for Malkin. The match exploded into life when Alex Rae was impeded in the area and dusted himself down to smash home the equaliser in the 64th minute from the penalty spot.

It had already been a quite remarkable match in terms of off-the-pitch activities that were more slapstick than sinister. A booming clearance from Lions' centre back Tony Witter not only cleared row Z but went all the way through a stadium window, sending shards of glass in all directions and the match was also provided with an impromptu commentary when a fan managed to not only gain access to, but lock himself in the PA announcer's booth and give a blow by blow account of the action over the Elm Park airwaves before the local constabulary forced access and ended this latest comical twist. Meanwhile back on the pitch, Kerry Dixon completed a fairy tale comeback by slotting home to give The Lions the lead. Unfortunately, as so often happens, this particular Millwall fairy tale was about to turn grim.

Rae was red-carded soon after the Dixon goal following a tussle with Gooding and Reading 'keeper Simon Shepard appeared to have an object thrown at him from the visiting fans' Town End terrace behind him. On inspection the object turned out to be a spanner and so the headlines for the following day were written. Rather than Millwall's third win in four ending Reading's unbeaten start and taking them back to the top of the table, talk once again was of if and how Millwall should be punished. It wasn't ideal preparation for the next away trip to Portsmouth.

3

Flattering to deceive

September 1995
Boxer Frank Bruno wins the WBC world heavyweight
championship; Colombia goalkeeper Rene Higuita
performs his trademark scorpion kick as Terry
Venables` England side face the south Americans
in a 0-0 draw at Wembley; A 15-year-old fan is
banned indefinitely from The Den after being
identified as the spanner-throwing fan during
Millwall's match at Reading. The club escape any
further punishment...

Millwall travelled to Fratton Park, scene of
their 6-1 humiliation which led to manager
Bruce Rioch leaving three years before,
looking to cement their place at the top of the Division
One table. Portsmouth wasn't just an unhappy ground in
recent seasons for The Lions. In 42 meetings since the
war, Millwall had managed just nine wins, with their last
success away coming almost a quarter of century before
in 1972.

Uwe Fuchs once again had to be content with a place on
the bench as Kerry Dixon was now making it impossible
for manager McCarthy not to start him and he once again
proved his goalscoring worth on the road with his third
winner in three trips. It was a scruffy goal in the 17th minute

of a scruffy game but the travelling Millwall supporters who were once again in fine voice following their triumphant midweek trip to Reading weren't complaining. The fact that a struggling Pompey side had made Millwall sweat on their lead on numerous occasions didn't ring any alarm bells with The Lions faithful - even the most cynical of whom were starting to believe that this season's Division One didn't hold many challenges to their claim on the title.

This belief was further bolstered when news came through of how their next opponents Barnsley had fared. Danny Wilson's side had been humiliated 5-0 at home by Birmingham and would surely not be relishing a trip into the league leader's Den the following Saturday.

That heavy Brum battering had however been a coupon-busting blip of its own in a season that was already panning out to be a worthy candidate for the script of the hit TV show at the time. The X Files saw agents Mulder and Scully in hot pursuit of the paranormal and unexplained but even they would have been hard pressed to fathom how events unfolded in Millwall's next match at The Den.

With barely 90 seconds on the clock and Millwall - with Fuchs making his first start of the season in place of the struggling Malkin - looking to get an early grip on the game, Redfearn gave Barnsley a lead. For the remaining 88 minutes of the game the Yorkshire side managed to reduce the combined efforts of an expensive - and experienced - Lions strikeforce to barely a whiff of a goal as they pulled off a classic smash and grab raid.

If Malkin's fruitless introduction as a 63rd minute substitute for the tiring Dixon in that latest Den disappointment had McCarthy and Millwall's fans worried that the former Tranmere man was struggling to settle in SE16, there was finally some relief to be had four days later.

After again being brought on with 30 minutes left in an

attempt to break the deadlock at home to struggling Luton, the sense of relief for player, team, fans and management was palpable when Malkin struck a last-minute winner to send Millwall back to the top of the table and end a frustrating little run of misfires on home turf.

The programme for the match picked up on a story in a recent edition of The Daily Mirror's finance section which recommended having a punt on Millwall shares. Whilst they had plummeted to just 2p each, the article picked up on The Lions' promotion credentials and the increasing wealth of the Premier League which would surely give the market value a big boost should the club reach the promised land. It was an optimism that had faded quite quickly on the terraces it seemed since that win at Portsmouth with barely 7,000 at The Den to witness another performance against a very ordinary side that flattered to deceive.

McCarthy, in typical straight-talking style, didn't pull any punches:

"The game was awful, we were awful" was his post-match assessment and he won't have needed reminding that his expensively assembled strike duo of £750,000 Fuchs and £450,000 Malkin were struggling to make an impression and, were it not for the goals of veteran Dixon - who himself had struggled since McCarthy tried to shoe-horn the German front man into the line-up in an attempt to kick-start his season, Millwall would be alongside Luton looking at the wrong end of the table.

Attacking shortcomings were still in evidence in the next two matches - but with the saving grace of not conceding at the other end. The unbeaten away league run continued at Norwich and Premier League Everton were held to a goalless Den draw in the first leg of a Coca Cola League Cup second round tussle.

Despite the top flight opposition attraction, Millwall's

lack-lustre performances were failing to inspire their fans as just over 12,000 witnessed Joe Royle's Merseyside giants held in SE16. Worse was to follow when Sunderland left with all three points in a fairly routine 2-1 victory despite the return of Alex Rae following his suspension for that altercation in the fiery encounter at Reading.

It didn't take long for Rae's return to have an impact however when he gave The Lions an early lead in the next match away to struggling Derby. The Rams who had managed just two wins so far were quickly back on level terms but Millwall finally seemed to have found the goal trail courtesy of debutant Kingsley Black who fired them back in front just before half time.

The Nottingham Forest winger signed on loan the previous week and looked to be providing the ammunition so badly lacking in previous games. Malkin and Fuchs continued to fire blanks however and there was a certain feeling of inevitability when Robin Van Der Laan made it 2-2 midway through the second half.

The away goals continued to flow however - and in spectacular fashion - as Millwall travelled to Goodison for the second instalment of their Coca Cola League Cup second round clash.

A goalless first half gave no indication of the drama to come and when a Hinchcliffe penalty and Stuart strike within nine minutes of the restart made it 2-0 to Everton, Millwall's first cup exit of the season was on the cards. That is until a young striker took control of proceedings.

Scott Taylor was a 19-year-old goalscoring prospect signed from non-league Staines Town in the summer but his arrival had understandably remained off the radar amid the fanfare of Fuchs' and Malkin's arrivals. Coming on as a 40th minute substitute for Thatcher, Taylor was first to react when Fuchs was dispossessed on the edge of the

Everton penalty area to stroke home.

Suddenly Millwall were playing their most attractive football of the season with Rae and Savage pulling all the strings in midfield and Taylor's pace off the last man causing the Everton defence constant trouble.

It was one such inch-perfect throughball from Savage that had home defender Earl Barrett reaching desperately to prevent another dangerous Taylor foray and his pace was too much for the ex-Oldham stalwart. Taylor tumbled and Alex Rae gleefully slotted home the penalty to make it 2-2 and send the match to extra time.

If Taylor's impact had bamboozled Everton in normal time, his next contribution in the added thirty minutes would have them shocked to their core. Another brilliant run and pass from Savage found Dixon on the right hand side and he found Taylor midway inside the Everton penalty area with his back to goal. Turning his marker, he let fly with an explosive shot that fizzed past the veteran Neville Southall and into the net to give Millwall the lead.

Savage deservedly put the gloss on an incredible result when he stroked home to make it 4-2 and seal one of Millwall's best cup performances since a 2-0 FA Cup win at the same venue some 22 years before.

Taylor's headline-grabbing exploits at Goodison meant McCarthy had to retain him in the new look 4-3-3 line-up for the next league match - a trip to Watford. It was rough on Kingsley Black who had been unable to feature in the cup match and had made such a great start to his loan spell but McCarthy was keen to keep a winning side and this was vindicated when Alex Rae struck a superb 68th minute winner at Vicarage Road.

In the build up to the next match the club announced the sad but somewhat unsurprising news that veteran defender Ian Dawes was to retire from the game.

Dawes had been an instant favourite with fans since his arrival at the start of the club's historic top flight debut back in 1988 and had served the club superbly throughout.

His final season had been punctuated by injury and limited to just 20 appearances - half of which Dawes openly admitted he shouldn't have played in. He struggled through the pain barrier to play a part in a thrilling FA Cup run which culminated in a penalty shoot out win against Chelsea at Stamford Bridge to set up what would have been a fairy tale finale in the next round against his original club QPR.

Sadly Dawes's body wasn't up to it and the curtain finally came down on an illustrious Lion's career.

Three encouraging away performances - and at last some goals - provided the perfect boost for McCarthy's stuttering side but that soft underbelly was once again in evidence at home when Tranmere visited. Millwall's once impregnable defence was starting to look flimsy as Moore gave the Wirral club a second half lead. Millwall were given a way back into the match just minutes later when referee Rob Harris awarded the home side a penalty which Dixon converted for his first home goal of the season to add to his early away winners.

With the clock running down, it looked as though more precious home points would be squandered until Keith Stevens struck a rare goal to seemingly snatch all three. Tranmere weren't finished however and Harris was once more pointing to the spot, this time at the other end and Gary Bennett happily accepted the chance to nick a late, late point for Rovers.

With twelve matches played, Millwall were nicely placed in second spot, but with at least half a dozen home points arguably wasted, it could - and should - have been so much better.

Millwall desperately needed their new strike force to start scoring, and what better time to do it than in the live televised next match: away to Crystal Palace.

After that, the next two matches would be the first real test of their promotion mettle. West Bromwich Albion would visit The Den and then a trip to St Andrews to face Birmingham City would see The Lions face up to two genuine promotion rivals. After a steady if unspectacular start to the season, things were about to get serious.

Endsleigh League Division One - October 15th 1995						
	P	W	D	L	F	A	PTS
1. Leicester	12	6	4	2	19	14	22
2. MILLWALL	**12**	**6**	**4**	**2**	**13**	**9**	**22**
3. WBA	12	6	3	3	17	12	21
4. Sunderland	12	5	5	2	14	11	20
5. Birmingham	12	5	4	3	20	13	18

4

Storming the Palace

October 1995...
Eric Cantona returns to the Manchester United
team after serving his eight month suspension
following his kung-fu kick at Crystal Palace;
Barnsley fans and stewards are accused of racism
following the Coca Cola match with Arsenal;
Cliff Richard is knighted;
Julie Goodyear (alias Bet Lynch) leaves Coronation
Street...

Trips to Selhurst Park were always virtual home
matches for Millwall as far as atmosphere was
concerned. Opinion was very much divided among
Lions fans as to Palace's true London rival credentials,
many still seeing West Ham as the club's truest adversary.
However, rivalry is often cultivated not just by proximity
but regularity of confrontation and sometimes by incident.

Older Millwall supporters will point to their somewhat
tamer neighbours from the leafy Croydon suburbs being
barely considered rivals at all until a fateful day at The Den
in the late 1960s when both teams were vying for a place in
the top flight for the first time.

Bert Head's Palace visited The Den in November 1968
still smarting from a 5-0 thrashing at the hands of The Lions
at the end of the previous season. With both sides in reach

of the Second Division promotions places, it may have been too early in the season to be deemed a six-pointer but Palace were clearly keen to settle old scores and send out a message to the rest of the division.

Their roughhouse tactics during a bad-tempered 2-0 victory boiled over when a cynical challenge on Millwall's Billy Neil resulted in the Lions' stalwart being substituted. Worse was to follow in the return match later that season when Neil was once again singled out. Palace completed the double over Millwall with a 4-2 win at Selhurst Park on that occasion and went on to win promotion. Neil meanwhile was ruled out for the rest of the season and played only 29 matches for the club over the next three seasons in stark contrast to almost 200 in the previous five.

I should point out that I am in no way stating the case for any rivalry between Millwall and Crystal Palace being the result of that season's encounters, this is purely anecdotal and many fans will be blissfully unaware of it - even those that were there that day.

Rivalries do manifest themselves from such incidents though - and similarly, Palace's curious obsession with Brighton can be pinpointed by the seventies spats between the two sides as they both climbed from Third to First Divisions under the charismatic leadership of Allison and Mullery.

It's understandable that most Millwall fans will always consider West Ham their main rival - and history supports this. But with meetings between the two so rare, and some lively battles with Palace for a decade following Millwall's FA Cup replay win in 1985, a younger generation had come to build the fixture into something with a little more spice - even if the intensity didn't extend to both home and away enclosures. On an unusually pleasant early Autumn Sunday in south east London, Brian Moore and his ITV

London Match team were there for live coverage. As the legendary commentator went through the line-ups - noting that Palace's three man defence included former Millwall prospect Andy Roberts - he did so to a deafening backdrop more familiar at Old Trafford than Selhurst Park.

A loud chorus of "Ooh ah, Eric Cantona" was being belted out by the boisterous Lions fans who, as usual for the fixture, seemed to occupy pockets of all four sections of the stadium in addition to the packed away end. As a support, Millwall fans often frown upon even modifications of terrace chants that other supporters sing, but allowances are always made in the name of taking the piss.

Here they were only too happy to remind Palace of the infamous incident that shook the football world nine months before when Eric Cantona launched himself into the crowd in response to fan Matthew Simmonds' abuse of the Frenchman.

The din extended to kick-off and beyond and was quickly amplified when a fantastic run from ex-Palace man Bobby Bowry saw the midfielder deliver a pinpoint cross to the waiting Chris Malkin who bulleted his header beyond Martyn in the Palace goal to give Millwall a second minute lead and spark pandemonium all around.

Lost in the moment, fellow striker Uwe Fuchs turned to the celebrating Millwall fans to offer a two-armed gee-up, maybe asking for them to crank it up to eleven, only to be greeted by one who took the invitation personally, scrambled onto the Selhurst Park pitch and moved in for a hug from the big German.

Frustratingly though, despite the intensity being maintained in the stands, Millwall were unable to build on that great start and just after the half hour mark Dean Gordon powered Palace level. The fact that the goal appeared to turn down the volume in the stadium spoke volumes about the variation in support from the two teams.

Undeterred, Millwall came back at Palace and within three minutes were back in front. Martyn flapped at a Van Blerk corner as Malkin moved in for his second and the ball fell kindly for Fuchs - who must have known very little about it as it bobbled into the net and sent the away fans delirious once more. As the stewards struggled to stem another mini pitch invasion, Fuchs set off on a goal celebration that would become part of the programme's opening titles for the rest of the season. It was straight out of the continental celebratory manual - complete with badge kiss - as chants of "Uwe" filled the air before the customary EIOs.

Palace, who before the match had managed just two wins in their previous ten matches, put up little resistance for the remainder of the match and whilst Millwall will have been slightly disappointed not to add to the score, on all other counts it had been perfect. For a start, it looked as though the controversial and much criticised transfer of Andy Roberts in return for the Palace duo of Newman and Bowry had certainly fallen in The Lions' favour. Both players had been outstanding and Roberts - a lifelong Lions fan from a family of Millwall supporters, cut a very solemn figure in his uncustomary central defensive role for the ragged Eagles. Millwall's expensively-assembled strikeforce had also seemingly proved their worth at last, to see both on the scoresheet will have been almost as satisfying as the Division One league table that evening:

Endsleigh League Division One - October 22nd 1995	P	W	D	L	F	A	PTS
1. Leicester	13	7	4	2	22	15	25
2. MILLWALL	13	7	4	2	15	10	25
3. WBA	13	7	3	3	19	13	24
4. Birmingham	13	6	4	3	22	13	22
5. Sunderland	13	5	6	2	15	12	21

The other end made for entertaining reading too:

	P	W	D	L	F	A	PTS
20. Crystal Palace	12	3	5	4	13	15	14
21. Luton	13	3	3	7	10	15	12
22. Sheffield Utd	13	3	2	8	17	25	11
23. Port Vale	13	2	5	6	11	16	11
24. Portsmouth	13	2	4	7	15	21	10

Millwall didn't have too long to enjoy their victory at Palace. Just three days later they were back in action at The Den where top flight Sheffield Wednesday were the visitors for a League Cup tie. This time, as at Palace, some Millwall supporters decided to display their emotions by joining the players on the pitch. Unfortunately on this occasion, it wasn't in celebration.

5

TOP CATS

Millwall were boring. It had to be said, there was no denying it. The win at Palace had been fun, sure, but mainly because of the atmosphere generated by the fans. The thing is, fans will take boring if it's winning football matches. Well they would back in 1995 anyway. In the modern era, where football is dissected and analysed to within an inch of its life, winning simply isn't enough. But Millwall fans had spent too many seasons watching their side be the most impressive not to get promoted to the top flight now. If they had to bore their way to The Premier League then so be it.

Cup matches were also a minor irritant (aside from that remarkable win at Everton) and so it was proving as another borefest unravelled in a 2-0 League Cup loss at home to Sheffield Wednesday. So a couple of Millwall's suffering denizens decided to liven things up a bit.

Two fans made their way onto The Den pitch with one confronting visiting goalkeeper Kevin Pressman. According to Pressman, the fan threatened him with the words: "You are a dead man. You will never leave this ground alive." The club moved quickly to limit the damage with the ramifications of the Derby play-off match still fresh in the memory and, as the FA confirmed they would be investigating, the club immediately banned the two fans for life. This time, without the unflappable Reg Burr to act as the club spokesman in the wake of such drama, Chief Executive Graham Hortop gave a less defensive statement than Burr was inclined to in recent years:

"Sadly, two of our supporters decided to make fools of themselves by going on to the pitch. The club will not tolerate such behaviour and have acted immediately by banning the two persons involved from The Den for life."

His public disdain was understandable. With the spanner incident just weeks before at Reading and now this, the threat of the £100,000 fine and two-match ground closure which literally hung over the club as the suspended punishment for the Derby trouble was too grim to contemplate, just as things were starting to look up for the club.

The press were no doubt dusting off their "Please God don't let Millwall win promotion" headlines three days later when promotion rivals West Brom visited The Den in what would be Millwall's first real test of their bid to climb into the big time - and both players and fans passed it with flying colours. Another disappointing attendance of less than 10,000 witnessed - from the stands this time - the Malkin/Fuchs goalscoring partnership hit the target for the second league match in a row. It may not have been a duo that tripped off the tongue like Cas and Teddy or Shearer and Sutton, but they were doing the business and, thanks to Leicester's unlikely 2-3 loss to Palace, Millwall were top cats at last:

Endsleigh League Division One - October 29th 1995						
	P	W	D	L	F	A	PTS
1. MILLWALL	14	8	4	2	17	11	28
2. Birmingham	14	7	4	3	24	14	25
3. Leicester	14	7	4	3	24	18	25
4. WBA	14	7	3	4	20	15	24

A Steve Claridge-inspired Birmingham were the next opponents. Millwall rarely fared well at St Andrews and older fans were already starting to have flashbacks of that heartbreaking season of 1971/72 when the midlands side pipped them to a top flight place, but McCarthy's Lions now had a fantastic opportunity to open up a lead at the top.

6

SQUEAKY BRUM TIME

November 1995...
Wolves manager Graham Taylor resigns;
Blackburn's David Batty and Graeme Le Saux argue
on the pitch during their side's 3-0 Champions
League defeat to Spartak Moscow;
Today – the first full-colour newspaper ceases
production after nine years;
Princess Diana's interview with Martin Bashir is
shown on BBC 1;
Rose West is found guilty of murdering ten women
and children...

The stage was set for early fireworks as Millwall
played their first match as Division One leaders
against a Birmingham side right behind them
on November 4th. The white hot atmosphere was inten-
sified by the packed away end which was swelled due to
the travelling Millwall fans being able to pay on the door.
Millwall had requested the match be made all-ticket but
Birmingham Chief Executive Karren Brady declined the
request meaning fans continued to pour in despite there
being little space in the seated area. With home fans seated
in the tier above them it felt like only a matter of time
before the blue touch paper was lit.

On the pitch Millwall started nervously and a defensive

mix-up almost allowed Claridge to curl the home side into an early lead. Ricky Otto was causing the Millwall defence all sorts of problems with his pace and trickery and should have made it 1-0 when, with only Keller to beat, he decided to try and take it around the American stopper only for his shot to be cleared off the line.

McCarthy had opted for an attacking line-up rather than play for a draw with young Scott Taylor playing in an attacking midfield role alongside Alex Rae behind the on-form strike duo of Malkin and Fuchs. A great Malkin run played Taylor in for Millwall's first chance but the youngster was unable to reproduce the stunning finishing he displayed at Goodison earlier in the season and he blazed a good chance over the bar and into the packed away section.

The inevitable happened however soon after when a Hunt free kick on the left hand side just outside the Millwall penalty area was headed home by Castle and the sides went into the half time break having swapped places in the league table - a fact that the raucous home fans ensured Lions fans were in no doubt about.

With chants of "We are top of the league" still echoing around St Andrews, Kerry Dixon, on as a half time sub for the injured Fuchs, provided the perfect response. A fantastic run by Van Blerk set up Taylor whose shot looked goal-bound but was tipped around the post for a corner and from the resulting set piece Malkin nodded Van Blerk's deep cross back across the face of goal for Dixon to head home with unerring ruthlessness.

Millwall were well on top now and pressed for a match winner but Birmingham held on until another corner was awarded on that same right hand side with just five minutes left. This time Van Blerk opted to play it short to the on-rushing Alex Rae. The Scot took a touch and hit a shot from the corner of the penalty area through a crowd of legs. Caught unaware, the Birmingham defence could only watch in horror as the ball took a bounce on the edge of the six yard box and nestled in the back of the net.

Now it was the Millwall fans' turn to remind home fans of the league placings and with third and fourth placed Leicester and West Brom facing each other 24 hours later, Millwall, for now at least, had a six point lead at the top of the Division One table, but there was inevitably one more twist in this thrilling clash.

With the final two minutes of the match ticking down, an innocuous looking cross by Poole into the Millwall box looked to have evaded any Birmingham player but the usually dependable Lions centre back Tony Witter failed to control the ball as he attempted to clear it to safety and, to his horror, it fell perfectly for Blues' striker Ken Charlery who couldn't quite believe his luck and all he had to do was slot the ball past a flat-footed Keller from inside the six yard box.

Millwall were still top, but it was a frustrating two points to squander after looking so comfortable against an in-form side just behind them in the table. Leicester's 3-2 win over West Brom instead saw them nestle up behind The Lions just a point behind but Witter was able to instantly atone for his St Andrews error when, back at The Den, he scored the winner in a 2-1 win over Ipswich. Malkin was once again on the scoresheet and a more healthy attendance of 11,360 started to believe that Millwall were building a solid, if unremarkable, promotion campaign.

It was the unremarkable aspect that would haunt them again though in the next home game when Huddersfield frustrated another sub-10,000 home crowd by taking a point back to Yorkshire in a 0-0 draw. Manager McCarthy opened his programme notes admitting that he'd take a one goal win every week - which was just as well because so far that was the only margin Millwall had managed to win by.

The problem with that is sooner or later the goals dry up and wins turn to draws - and then defeats.

That seemed to be the pattern three days later as a midweek trip to Oldham looked like condemning Millwall to the first loss in almost two months and a first away from home of the season. Stuart Barlow made it 2-0 to The Latics with just ten minutes left but the hardy souls who had made the long trip from south London to the freezing north west were given an unlikely thawing out when they were able to celebrate goals from Rae and Malkin in the last five minutes to snatch a point - and keep Millwall at the summit going into the upcoming trip to Stoke.

As Millwall fans gathered on the old Victoria Ground's away end, all the talk was of another new defensive addition to Mick McCarthy's squad making his debut. Gerard Lavin had signed for The Lions for a reported fee of around £500,000 - a huge and unprecedented outlay for a Lions back four player. Arriving from Watford, the highly-rated Scottish right back slotted straight into the starting lineup at Stoke, with Ricky Newman - who in Lions fans' eyes hadn't really done anything wrong - dropping to the bench.

The move came out of the blue but was encouraging news for supporters who watched their side start the match with just one defeat in their last twelve league games but the news turned bad as a goal from Nigel Gleghorn was enough to inflict Millwall's first away defeat of the season.

7

Wear and tear and farewell to army

December 1995...
Wolves want Leicester manager Mark McGhee but
are refused permission to speak to him;
England are drawn in the same group as Scotland
for the Euro 96 tournament;
McGhee walks out on Leicester to join Wolves;
Jack Charlton resigns as manager of Ireland;
Altnaharra in the Scottish Highlands matches the
lowest temperature UK Weather Record at -27.2;
Riots break out in Brixton after the death of
26-year-old, Wayne Douglas in police custody...

Mick McCarthy bemoaned his side's sloppy defending in both the Oldham and Stoke matches in his programme notes for the next home match against struggling Watford, declaring that Lavin "would have better matches than that" and was "good enough for The Premier League" should Millwall make it there.

If Lavin's start to life with The Lions was a slight disappointment, at least one of McCarthy's other recruits was really starting to show promise. Malkin scored his fifth goal in eight games on the stroke of half time of the clash with The Hornets. Unfortunately for him and another disappointing Den crowd, Watford had already scored twice and held on through the second period to claim a 2-1 win and condemn The Lions to back to back defeats.

Somehow Millwall were still top of the table but hanging on by a thread with Sunderland behind them by virtue of less goals scored - which was some feat given how hard The Lions were finding it to hit the back of the net. The trip to Roker Park in four days' time was looking like a banker 0-0 draw based on the two sides' shot-shy form, but first there was the small matter of maintaining their long-running good form against local rivals Charlton who arrived at a snow-swept Den for a midweek encounter for what should have been an easy return to winning ways.

After the worst possible preparation and speculation already building that Ireland were keen to interview Mick McCarthy for the now vacant manager's job following Jack Charlton's resignation, Millwall fans could only look on in horror as a goal in each half from Kim Grant sent The Lions spinning to a third defeat in a row - and only the second home defeat to Charlton since the war. Even in the icy conditions Charlton were able to waltz almost unchallenged through the Millwall defence for both goals in a match that finished 10 v 10 with Keith Stevens and Lee Bowyer receiving their marching orders

Despite this inexplicable loss in form, Millwall arrived in the north east still at the top of the table and determined to re-establish their cushion with a win at Sunderland. Instead, what transpired in the next ninety minutes at Roker Park sent The Lions' season into freefall.

With just fifteen minutes on the clock an already unsettled Millwall side were caught on the back foot and veteran defender Anton Rogan felled Phil Gray in the box. Martin Scott calmly stroked home the spot kick and with that Millwall's season began to unravel in spectacular fashion.

Striker Craig Russell mad it 2-0 on the half hour mark and

any hopes that Millwall's travelling fans had of a repeat of the comeback witnessed at Oldham a few weeks before were quickly dashed as goals from Gray and Russell made it 4-0 after just 58 minutes. Russell who was having the game of his life - aided by an increasingly generous Millwall defence - completed his treble soon after and rubbed The Lions' noses in it with his fourth in the last minute. Three of the four second half goals came from the Millwall right and whilst it was unfair to lay the blame of such an inept all-round team display at the feet of one player, fans were understandably starting to point to the arrival of Gerard Lavin as the turning point in Millwall's season. Since his debut at Stoke Millwall record read: played four, lost four, with eleven goals conceded and just one scored.

A shell-shocked Millwall trudged from the pitch after one of their worst defeats in decades, their promotion credentials in tatters. If they had been courting Lady Luck by remaining top of the table through that run of defeats she had now deserted them completely. In 90 punishing minutes on Wearside, The Lions had been transformed from Championship contenders into play-off also-rans. After leading the table at the start of the day, they ended it down in seventh position:

Endsleigh League Division One - December 12th 1995						
	P	W	D	L	F	A	PTS
1. Sunderland	20	10	5	3	28	15	37
2. Derby	21	9	7	5	34	27	34
3. Norwich	21	9	7	5	32	23	34
4. Birmingham	21	9	7	5	32	25	34
5. Stoke	21	9	7	5	31	24	34
6. Grimsby	21	9	7	5	26	23	34
7. MILLWALL	22	9	7	5	24	27	34

Of course, the optimist would look at it as joint second, but that would be papering over the cracks that, in just four

games had become gaping holes that McCarthy was struggling to plug. To say nothing of the morale of the team that,
by Alex Rae's admission, had been shot to pieces during
that horror show at Sunderland. In a division that was
wide open, Millwall should have been looking down on
the rest going into the festive period. Following the tried
and trusted promotion formula would have seen them on
42 points at this stage - a seven point lead over second
placed Sunderland and eight clear of the third place outside
automatic promotion. No one team was taking the division
by the scruff of the neck - perfectly illustrated by Stoke and
Grimsby's arrival in the promotion-chasing pack. Even
Millwall's hopes of usurping their rivals on the same points
total was rendered impossible for the foreseeable future as
their goal difference had been plunged into a negative as a
result of that crushing 6-0 defeat - a fact compounded by
their goalscoring record which was by far the worst in the
top seven. It was hardly the best preparation for the visit of
second-placed Derby next.

In typical fashion, McCarthy joked in his programme
notes for the game:

*"If we went through everything that went wrong at
Sunderland last weekend we wouldn't have time to prepare
for the games in February matches, let alone the one here
this afternoon..."*

He revealed that, on the training ground, they had gone
back to basics and were looking at reverting to a more solid
4-4-2 formation. But it didn't work.

A 44th-minute goal by Sturridge was enough to give
Derby one of their easiest wins of the season and send
Millwall spinning down to tenth. Their ascent to the top
of the table had been slow, arduous but the result of hard
work and grinding out results. The fall from their perch had
been spectacular and swift. Since hitting the heights with

that Malkin and Fuchs-inspired 2-1 win over promotion rivals West Brom less than two months before, Millwall had surrendered time and again with just six points taken from a possible 27. Fuchs was once again a bit part player with Kerry Dixon although there was a brief glimmer of hope when they travelled to relegation-haunted Wolves on Boxing Day and a Malkin goal rescued a point with ten minutes left.

Wolves had also been suffering. Under immense pressure to win promotion, they had started the season badly and sacked ex-England boss Graham Taylor. After casting an envious eye across the midlands at promotion-chasing Leicester they made an audacious approach for Foxes' manager Mark McGhee.

McGhee had quickly built a reputation as one of the top young managers in the game when, in his first post, he led Reading to a storming promotion to the second tier which prompted Leicester to put him in charge of their bid for the top flight. It was all going according to plan as Leicester led the division ahead of Millwall in the opening weeks and they understandably refused Wolves' approach for their relatively new boss. To the shock of their fans and board, McGhee then walked out on high-flying Leicester to take the Wolves job. Leicester then mirrored Millwall's fall from early season grace and drifted to mid-table while McGhee struggled to work the same magic at Molineux.

Leicester would be Millwall's first opponents of 1996. The match at The Den was an opportunity to start afresh, with just four points between The Lions in tenth and Charlton in second there was still a chance to reignite that promotion push.

Another opportunity to revitalise their bid for promotion would come in the shape of more new signings, two players who would arrive at The Den in a wave of publicity and establish themselves in Millwall folklore for years to come - but for all the wrong reasons.

Meanwhile, the rumours about Mick McCarthy being very much in the frame for the Ireland job had started to gather momentum, even if, to the annoyance of the Millwall board and fans, nothing concrete appeared to have been discussed (certainly neither party were confirming so) and therefore the opportunity to dismiss it and get on with breathing life into Millwall's season was being hindered. As the Mark McGhee situation had proved however, even a rebuff from the Millwall board to the FAI's advances was no guarantee, and that breath of life was soon to turn into gasps for air.

A year that had shown so much promise ended on a far sadder note than mere football results can convey however when it was announced on December 29th that legendary Millwall defender Harry Cripps had passed away after suffering a heart attack at the relatively young age of 54.

Cripps transcended the bitter rivalry of Millwall and West Ham when, after serving his apprenticeship with The Hammers, he joined Millwall after appearing in the 1958/59 FA Youth Cup final alongside Bobby Moore and quickly went on to become a cult hero with The Lions fans.

He made his debut in August 1961 against Wrexham and became an integral part of a Millwall side that enjoyed successive promotions from Division Four to Division Two and created the then Football League record of 59 league matches undefeated at home. He came agonisingly close to completing the journey from league basement to top flight when he was part of Benny Fenton's brilliant 1971/72 team that missed out on promotion by the most dramatic of margins.

After 14 seasons of loyal service to The Lions he left for Charlton in 1974 by which time he had amassed a record-breaking 400 league appearances for The Lions, beating the record of Jimmy Forsyth of 321 Football League appearances.

He later became a coach at Crystal Palace, as well as assistant manager at Charlton and manager of Barking. He was also involved in coaching at Winchester College.

Harry Cripps
Born: Dereham, Norfolk, 29/4/1941
Height: 5ft 10ins
Position: Left back
Signed from:
West Ham (Free Transfer) 12/06/60
Transferred to:
Charlton, October 1974
Millwall appearances: 443
(including 11 as sub)
Millwall goals: 39

SOUth BErmonDsey homesick BLUes

8

FUCHS Off

January 1996...
Kevin Keegan's Newcastle go nine points clear at
the top of the Premier League;
England coach Terry Venables to stand down after
the Euro 96 tournament;
Polls show Tony Blair's Labour Party have a lead
of 26 points over John Major's Conservatives with a
general election due in 1997...

There was continued green shoots of hope in
Millwall's first league game of 1996. Despite
falling behind to a Steve Corica goal out of
nowhere on the stroke of half time, Chris Malkin was again
on hand to level things up against Leicester and make it
two matches without loss. Those two matches may have
been drawn but it was a welcome respite from the string
of defeats that had knocked Millwall from top spot to mid
table in the blink of an eye.

The club was still reeling from the sudden passing of
Harry Cripps when Second Division Oxford visited The
Den for an FA Cup third round tie. Much of the programme
was quite rightly dedicated to the life of Cripps and tributes
from all quarters ahead of his funeral service five days later.

Some more news that had broken much too late to be
included in that edition was the arrival of two new signings,

but these weren't your average run-of-the-mill captures and, in amongst the shock realisation of the sudden passing of a club hero was equal waves of surprise at the news that Millwall had somehow secured the signature of what appeared to be two world class players on loan for the remainder of the season.

The day before the cup clash, Sergei Yuran and Vassili Kulkov arrived from Champions League regulars Spartak Moscow. Both Russian internationals, Kulkov was given the nickname 'the Russian Baresi' and striker Yuran had scored goals at the highest level for Benfica, Porto, Spartak and his national side.

After bidding farewell to a long-serving hero that was so typical of Millwall Football Club in Harry Cripps, Lions fans were now welcoming two new players that were totally alien to them - high profile, top flight, internationals with glowing reputation who could have reportedly walked into any number of Premier League teams at that time.

Before the pair could make their Millwall bows however, there was the small matter getting back to winning ways and back on the promotion trail for the rest of the squad. Surely lower league opposition would help ease The Lions back into the saddle?

After an eventful second half - where Alex Rae equalised Stuart Massey's first half opener - only for Paul Moody to restore Oxford's lead - McCarthy's men looked to have sneaked it when a leveller from Malkin and another from Rae made it 3-2 to Millwall with five minutes remaining. The visitors had other ideas however and Ford's injury time goal earned the Division Two side a replay.

Now all eyes were on Millwall for the following weekend's league match at The Den against struggling Port Vale and the eagerly-awaited unveiling of what was being described by the club as "the transfer coup of the season".

The match programme for the game went into great detail about how both manager McCarthy and chairman Peter Mead had spent the previous weeks in lengthy and complicated negotiations to pull off the surprise move:

"It would be fair to say that the football world was 'stunned' to say the least when Millwall announced the signing of Sergei Iouran (commonly pronounced Yuran) and Vassili Kulkov at a hastily convened Press Conference at The Den last Friday. Negotiations, which had lasted some three weeks, had taken place in the utmost secrecy, such that the press had no inkling of what was in the offing, and given the quality of the players in question, this was vital so as not to attract attention to their availability. Millwall Chairman Peter Mead rightly paid tribute to his Chief Executive Graham Hortop and assistant Yvonne Haines who had been at The Den until 2 o'clock in the morning on more than one occasion working on the complex deal which has ultimately seen Iouran and Kulkov join us on loan from Moscow Spartak until the end of the season, with the option to make the transfers permanent thereafter. "This is a great day for Millwall Football Club" enthused Mr Mead. "In forty five years as a Millwall fan I can't remember us ever signing two quality international players, let alone Russians, at the same time. I'm tremendously excited by their arrival, and I think if anyone needed convincing just how seriously ambitious we are this should do it." Lions boss Mick McCarthy was equally thrilled with the deal. "When somebody rang and started to leave a message on my answerphone to the effect that these two players were available, I was tempted just to let it run. But I picked up the phone and spoke to the person concerned and this led to three of the most nerve wracking weeks I've experienced for a long time, I'm very pleased that we've

been able to complete the deal and I'm looking forward to seeing Iouran and Kulkov in action. I'm convinced that they'll give us a tremendous boost." Peter Mead elaborated further on the complexity of the negotiations which led to so many sleepless nights over the festive period. "I can now understand why arms limitation agreements with the Russians took so long in the past. There were phone calls back and forth not only to Russia but to Colombia and other places, and on more than one occasion it looked as though the deal might fall through. But in the end we have been rewarded for being so quick off the mark in the first place and for our persistence. I'm sure that a number of other clubs would have been interested in these players if they had the chance. When Mick first told me that Iouran and Kulkov were available I was determined that we had to move hell or high water to try to bring them to Millwall, and thankfully we have been able to achieve that." Press reports had indeed linked Iouran with Arsenal and Newcastle in the past, and according to the South London Press, a top Spanish club had made an eleventh hour bid to snatch Kulkov from under Millwall's nose but to no avail. Certainly, ex-England boss Bobby Robson, who has been a friend of Mr Hortop since his Fulham days, proved a significant influence in recommending Millwall to the two players. Both had played for Robson's Porto side last season and helped them to the Portuguese League title. He had wanted to keep them for the new season but circumstances prevented it. However, he had no hesitation in providing assurances both to Millwall and to the Russians that their link up would prove mutually beneficial. Speaking through an interpreter, Iouran, who like Kulkov speaks very little English confirmed; "It has always been our ambition to play in English football, and although we did not know much about Millwall, Mr Robson told us that they were a good club with great potential. We have come here to try to help them win promotion this season." Although they have played for some of Europe's top sides, including Benfica as well as Porto and have played for Moscow Spartak in the Champions League this season, Iouran affirmed that he did not see the move to The Den as a step down. "The, standard of English football is very high, and I don't think there is too much difference between the Premiership and the First Division. The atmosphere at Millwall is very good and we are both very much looking forward to playing here." Not only have Iouran and Kulkov played at the top at club level, but both are established Russian internationals with 29 and 45 caps respectively and are certain to feature in the European Championships in England this summer. At 26 and 29 (sharing the same birthday, June 11th incidentally), Iouran and Kulkov are vastly experienced and are set to make their first Football League appearances this afternoon."

The move certainly had its desired effect on the attendance with over 14,000 at The Den to see the pair make their Millwall debuts - the highest home turnout of the season by far - but this, coupled with the fact that both went straight into The Lion's starting lineup, must have sent some murmurs of consternation around the stands as kick-off time approached.

Was this a genuine move to boost the team's promotion prospects or a publicity stunt to boost disappointing gate receipts? Was part of this complex deal a guarantee that both players must start all matches during their stay? How would this impact on a dressing room already trying to recover from a morale-sapping spell of just one win in their previous eleven matches?

The selection decision of at least one of the Russian

recruits was settled for now at least, and if Millwall fans had been shellshocked by this sudden Baltic blast they would have been blown away to see confirmation in that same programme that German striker Uwe Fuchs was off.

McCarthy revealed that Fuchs had signed for Fortuna Dusseldorf on loan for the rest of the season with the deal likely to become permanent in the summer. Whether the transaction was purely financial in order to oil the wheels of the signings of Yuran and Kulkov or simply because both parties had agreed things weren't working out was obviously not confirmed in the manager's brief explanation.

One thing for certain was that the side could not accommodate both Yuran and Fuchs and it would have been hugely unfair to drop Chris Malkin who was one of the few players whose form had seemingly come through that horror spell unscathed. Also not up for debate was the club wage bill which by now must have been starting to spiral sharply upwards.

There was no doubt that both Fuchs and Malkin would have been offered lucrative contracts quite possibly above more established first team regulars and top performers such as Alex Rae. If that had perpetuated a split in the dressing room, one can only ponder the possible fallout from the arrival of two new highly paid players with seemingly a free pass into the first team.

Rather than an exciting 'coup', this felt like an incredibly risky gamble and one that simply had to pay off, starting with victory over Port Vale.

A large crowd at The Den can work in one of two ways: it can act as the vaunted twelfth man and spur the team on to success, or it can leave the players in no doubt that they have failed. For Millwall at the moment, failure wasn't an option and yet, by the time referee Uriah Rennie brought the numbing 2-1 home defeat to Port Vale to it's conclusion, failure appeared to be a constant companion once more.

The visitors had taken an early lead through Martin Foyle - a player who seemed to have haunted The Lions for both Vale and previous club Oxford. Millwall were back in it thanks to an Alex Rae goal on the half hour but neither Kulkov or Yuran were able to inspire their new team to a much-needed victory and there was a familiar feeling of inevitability (and sound of seats being left) when Naylor won the game for the visitors in the second half.

Millwall's starting line-up for the game had two other noticeable absentees. Goalkeeper Kasey Keller was on international duty for the USA in the CONCACAF Cup and was replaced by Tim Carter and Gerard Lavin, the right back who had arrived with so much promise with The Lions sitting proudly at the top of the table, had been benched after loss number four - in his fourth appearance for the club.

Yuran and Kulkov were not included for the FA Cup replay at Oxford and the lack of surprise in the Second Division side's 1-0 victory which dumped The Lions out of the competition spoke volumes about the new low that Millwall's season had now plunged to. They did however start the next match away at Grimsby where two second half goals from Rae turned a half time deficit into a first win in almost three months. What made the win all the more remarkable was that it was a first Millwall victory at Blundell Park for 75 years.

Not only was the sense of relief around the club palpable, it was boosted by the promising performances of Yuran and Kulkov and both players' performances were lauded by McCarthy along with that of Rae whose relentless scoring ability from midfield had dug Millwall out of a hole yet again. Even more encouraging was that first win in eleven league attempts had catapulted The Lions from twelfth back up to a play-off place in what was still a highly congested and hotly contested Division One table.

The mood around the club finally appeared to be lifting and optimists could perhaps justifiably point to the fact that, of those eleven winless matches, four had been drawn and with the exception of the thrashing at Sunderland and rare home defeat to Charlton, they could consider themselves unlucky to have lost five by the odd goal. In all, six of those matches had been against teams now very much in the promotion frame. There appeared to be a return of the spark that was in evidence at the start of the season - coincidentally with a win over Grimsby. More importantly, damage had been limited and although Derby were starting to stretch clear at the top, second place was still very much in their sights - especially as it was occupied by Charlton.

The month ended as it had begun, with a 1-1 draw. A Van Blerk first half opener being cancelled out by Portsmouth's Deon Burton, but the feeling amongst fans - and it appeared players - was that the storm had been ridden out and, with their two world-class additions now seemingly settling in, it was time to focus firmly on 18 games to win promotion.

If Millwall fans thought their season was about to settle down however they were in for a nasty shock. Just days after that Portsmouth draw, Millwall were looking for a new manager.

9

a slippery slope

February 1996...
Birmingham found guilty of spectator misconduct
at their November match against Millwall and
ordered to play one game behind closed doors if
there is another incident;
Former Liverpool manager Bob Paisley dies aged 77;
Orient's Roger Stanislaus gets a one year ban for
drug abuse;
The IRA carry out the Docklands bombing, which
injures 39 people, kills two and ends the 17-month
ceasefire;
The Princess of Wales agrees to give The Prince
of Wales a divorce, more than three years after
separating...

The old cliché about a week being a long time in politics certainly rang true for a long weekend in football at Millwall. No sooner had Millwall surrendered meekly to a 2-0 defeat at in-form Southend, manager Mick McCarthy had announced his resignation as manager of The Lions and by Monday morning the world's worst kept secret was finally out of the bag when the FAI unveiled him as Ireland's new coach.

By February 8th McCarthy's seat was filled by Jimmy Nicholl the highly-rated manager of Scottish Premier Division Raith Rovers. Nicholl enjoyed meteoric success at Raith taking them into the top flight and overseeing a League Cup final win over giants Celtic and it was lauded - once more - by chairman Mead as a major coup. Almost as quickly as McCarthy departed and Nicholl arrived, major changes on the playing front happened. Uwe Fuchs had suddenly returned from his brief spell in Germany and came off the bench in that defeat at Southend to replace - somewhat ironically as his arrival seemed to have signalled Fuchs' departure - Yuran. The other half of the Russian contingent also saw their game time curtailed by substitution and by the time Nicholl's arrival was officially unveiled in the Millwall programme for the home match with Reading, both Kulkov and Yuran were conspicuous by their absence from the matchday squad.

Instead Lavin was restored to the starting line-up and youngster James Connor handed his third start after making his debut in McCarthy's final home game against Pompey. In their only programme notes of the briefest of caretaker manager spells, the two Ians (Evans and McDonald) spoke of their assurance that only players truly committed to Millwall would be given a shirt.

Reading between the lines with rumours already circulating about the Russians' conduct in the bright lights of London and their sudden absence from the starting line-up, one could only assume that the gamble had failed miserably. A fairly unremarkable 1-1 draw with Reading - where Palace recruits Newman and Bowry both managed to score (except Bowry found the net at the wrong end) was followed by back-to-back away defeats at Sheffield United and Luton with no goals scored.

Nicholl was having a baptism of fire so he must have been as relieved as the fans when, for his first official home game in charge against Norwich, not only did Bowry score at the correct end, but Uwe Fuchs celebrated his renaissance with the second goal to give Millwall a 2-1 win over their fellow mid-tablers from Norfolk.

Yuran had seemingly earned a small reprieve with a last-minute substitute appearance and the official word was that both Russians had been suffering injuries. Kulkov remained on the treatment table - although rumours were growing that both had been seeing more of the drinks cabinet than any other item of furniture. On the eve of that Norwich appearance Yuran was arrested for failing to provide a breath test, making his appearance all the more puzzling. Another tumultuous month came to a close at Barnsley where Yuran managed ninety unremarkable minutes and the Jimmy Nicholl honeymoon appeared to be well and truly over as the Yorkshire side eased to a 3-1 victory. If he thought he'd come to Millwall to reignite their promotion fire he was soon to find out that he was about to be trying to plug the holes in a sinking ship.

Endsleigh League Division One - February 29th 1996	P	W	D	L	F	A	PTS
6. Barnsley	32	12	11	9	43	46	47
7. Leicester	32	11	13	8	47	43	46
8. Crystal Palace	31	11	12	8	42	40	45
9. Southend	32	12	8	12	45	41	44
10. MILLWALL	**34**	**11**	**11**	**12**	**34**	**44**	**44**

March 1996...
Manchester United overhaul Newcastle's huge lead at the top of the Premier League to top the table; England unveil a controversial new grey change strip in their friendly win over Bulgaria at Wembley;
A gunman kills sixteen children, a teacher and himself in the Dunblane massacre. The killer is quickly identified as 43-year-old former scout leader Thomas Hamilton. It is the worst killing spree in the United Kingdom since the Hungerford massacre in 1987...

Jimmy Nicholl had built a reputation for giving youth a chance and sure enough, young Australian prospect Lucas Neill was given his senior debut in that defeat at Luton and he made his home debut for Nicholl's first win at home to Norwich. Tony Dolby had also made a reappearance. He had been something of a forgotten man since bursting into the first team from the youth set-up some four years previously. Nicholl insisted he was making team selections based on the commitment he witnessed in training. Nicholl was going to need more than just blood and sweat though if he was to avoid the tears with crunch matches against Charlton and Crystal Palace looming on the horizon.

The Russian experiment took another disastrous turn when Yuran was dismissed late in the next home defeat to Wolves and once more three points were surrendered to a side lurking ominously just below Millwall bringing the trip to play rivals Charlton seven days later sharply into focus.

Since their historic victory at The Den back in December, Charlton had kept their momentum and were handily placed in third just behind Sunderland and eight points clear of Millwall who were now back in tenth. Defeat at The Valley would end Millwall's already feint automatic promotion hopes. The fear now wasn't points totals but matches played.

The Lions had played two, three and in some cases four matches more than many of the teams around them. With them being close to the bottom of the form table, whilst Nicholl continued to talk up prospects of regaining a place in those all-important play-off places, the reality was that, if his side didn't pull themselves out of their nosedive, they could easily find themselves stuck in a relegation battle.

If Nicholl was refusing to panic just one month into the job, the Millwall fans were certainly beginning to. Their trip to The Valley got off to the worst possible start - and had an equally disastrous finish as goals from Bowyer and Leaburn gave Charlton their first league double over The Lions since 1934 and sent Millwall into the bottom half of the table for the first time that season and closer to the relegation places than play-off ones.

There was no escaping the fact now that Millwall's target of promotion - even via the play-offs - was gone. They may have only been eight points from sixth-placed Huddersfield, but with just ten games remaining and Nicholl seemingly no closer to settling on his favoured starting line-up - or being able to put a side out capable of winning football matches, even the most optimistic of fans would have been hard pushed to expect anything other than a mid table finish. There was brief respite when a Fuchs goal earned a 1-0 home win over Sheffield United but defeat away to Leicester made it four defeats in five as they prepared to welcome Crystal Palace to The Den. Far from sparking a recovery, the signing of Yuran and Kulkov had seemingly robbed Millwall of one of their few consistent performers in Chris Malkin who had been a regular starter and finding the net until the January arrival of the Russian pair. Frozen out, a move to promotion-chasing Charlton was being negotiated but in-keeping with Millwall's farcical season, fell through leaving Nicholl with the prospect of reintro-ducing a clearly unhappy player into first team action. With Yuran still yet to score, the irony that Nicholl's best striking options were the ones the club had invested so heavily in at the start of the season was not lost on fans with Fuchs finally starting to find some form, had he been able to rekindle his partnership with Malkin there may have been some salvation in Millwall's season.

Palace's revival had been as sudden as Millwall's demise with the appointment of Dave Bassett as their manager following an early season struggle under the stewardship of Ray Lewington and Peter Nicholas. When Malkin and Fuchs had scored the goals at Selhurst Park to earn Millwall that impressive 2-1 win and take them to within touching distance of the top of the table, Palace were languishing at the opposite end. Now they had overtaken Charlton in third place and were breathing down the necks of a faltering Derby.

Nicholl's transfer deadline dealings had the distinct look of a man in trouble, Dale Gordon was signed on loan from West Ham and made his debut in the defeat at Leicester but it was a signing that failed to fill Lions fans with much enthusiasm.

Gordon had been a star performer at Norwich during that brief but golden era when Millwall and the Norfolk club had been considered contenders for the top flight title. Since then injury had blighted his career and he was hoping to rekindle it with a spell of games at The Den.

It was made clear to Nicholl that any more incoming transfer dealings would have to be done in conjunction with players leaving The Den. It was the first sign of the very dark days that lay ahead, but there were some equally dark times waiting for them right now.

Whilst goals from Palace's George Ndah in the closing minutes gave the scoreline a somewhat flattering look, there was no doubt, as Millwall's fans trudged away from The Den after witnessing a humiliating 4-1 capitulation to Palace, which of the two sides were going in which direction. The visitors had ridden their luck from the first whistle and yet were able to extend their run to just one defeat in twenty whilst Millwall's frightening descent towards the bottom three continued.

You had to feel sorry for Nicholl. He had been brought into a club with genuine promotion prospects and a team full of experienced pros - with a couple of internationals to boot. He would no doubt have needed time to assess his squad but, with them sitting reasonably pretty just a couple of wins outside the promotion shake-up, the job should have been a relatively straight-forward one with a target of at least a play-off place.

Now, with just seven matches left, he was facing a nail-biting battle with relegation with a team completely devoid of confidence, fragmented and in the worst form of the entire division.

SOuth Bermondsey homesick blues

10

COUNTING Chickens

April 1996...
FA slap 10-year ticket ban on Mick McCarthy for
selling on two Cup Final tickets which ended up on
the black market;
Newcastle manager Kevin Keegan holds his famous
"I will love it" interview with Sky Sports as the
Premier League title race goes down to the wire
with Fergie's Manchester United;
A different Fergie is also in the news as the Duke
and Duchess of York announce they are to divorce...

The celebrations from the stands at The Den as
referee Clive Wilkes brought Millwall's match
with Birmingham to an end would not have looked
out of place had they been celebrating promotion. A nerve-
jangling 2-0 victory had been secured courtesy of goals
from Bobby Bowry and Chris Malkin. Two of the players
brought in by Mick McCarthy the previous summer to help
mastermind Millwall's promotion campaign had scored the
goals which looked to have saved them from relegation.

Of course, mathematically Millwall still weren't safe
but that victory, following on from a useful point away to
Tranmere at the start of the month meant The Lions had
now reached 51 points - the target considered to be safe.

Bottom-of-the-table Watford were seemingly doomed

and whilst Luton, Oldham and Reading below them were on 41, 45 and 46 points respectively, Millwall had two games still to play at The Den and would certainly fancy their chances of making safety indisputable - especially as Oldham were next to visit.

A trip to Huddersfield awaited next however and they didn't help their preparations for that unlikely of relegation six-pointers against Oldham by getting beaten 3-0 by a Terriers side chasing a play-off spot. There was relief when news came in that Oldham had only managed a draw with Wolves, but Reading's victory over Barnsley meant that those post-match celebrations were maybe starting to look a little premature. Millwall could not afford to drop points against Oldham, defeat was unthinkable:

Endsleigh League Division One - April 17th 1996							
	P	W	D	L	F	A	PTS
19. MILLWALL	43	13	12	18	41	59	51
20. Reading	42	11	16	15	49	59	49
21. Portsmouth	43	12	12	19	60	68	48
22. Oldham	42	11	13	18	49	49	46
23. Luton	42	8	17	17	54	65	41
24. Watford	41	10	11	20	36	57	41

Whilst Luton joining their arch rivals Watford in almost certain relegation was good news - as was Portsmouth suddenly becoming involved in the scrap to avoid just one more relegation spot, there were two things very much working against The Lions.

Firstly, they had played more than two of their relegation rivals and secondly, with goal average rather than goal difference being the deciding factor should points be equal this season, it was clear that should it come down to that finest of margins, Jimmy Nicholl's Lions would be found wanting. There was precious little chance of making up the eight-goal shortfall they were conceding to both Reading and Oldham and certainly no way of overhauling Pompey's huge nineteen-goal advantage.

Mercifully it was very much in their own hands. Victory over Oldham would see Millwall on 54 points and leave The Latics needing to win all three of their remaining matches to reach 55. With Portsmouth also having three matches left to play - including tricky clashes with play-off hopefuls Huddersfield and Ipswich, one more win would almost certainly do it.

It's hard to conclude how a match could have gone more wrong. Whether it was the penalty conceded just after half time which Oldham's Richardson duly despatched or the dismissal of Alex Rae ten minutes from time - a straight red excluding him from the final game of the season away to Ipswich, which was looking increasingly likely to be the day Millwall's fate as a First Division side would be decided. The Lions had dominated Oldham almost from start to finish and yet squandered chance after chance. On one of the few forays into the Millwall penalty area the unlucky Tony Witter was guilty of conceding the all-important penalty. Witter was a fans' favourite for all the usual reasons that Millwall players enter into that privileged position: he was honest, hard-working and flawed. Fans could accept the occasional cock-up if they showed they cared - and there was never any doubt that Tony Witter did so very deeply.

The problem was, with games running out and the teams around them picking up points, any more slip-ups could take matters out of Millwall's hands. The unlikely scenario of The Lions losing all of their final four matches after what looked like a season-saving win at home to Birmingham was now scarily close. While Millwall were losing to Oldham, Portsmouth and Reading were drawing blanks with goalless draws against Barnsley and Charlton respectively so fortune was it seemed still slightly in Jimmy

Nicholl's favour. But they couldn't afford to rely on others any more. The final home match of a campaign that should have been flagged up for championship-winning celebrations akin to those at the old Den back in May 1988 was now a desperate final act to avoid a nerve-shredding final day at Ipswich.

Endsleigh League Division One - April 23rd 1996							
	P	W	D	L	F	A	PTS
19. MILLWALL	44	13	12	19	41	60	51
20. Reading	43	11	17	15	49	59	50
21. Portsmouth	44	12	13	19	60	68	49
22. Oldham	43	12	13	18	49	49	49
23. Watford	44	9	18	17	60	68	45
24. Luton	43	10	11	21	36	58	42

In what was proving to be one of the closest relegation battles in decades, even bottom-of-the-pile Luton could conceivably catch Millwall were they to win all three of their remaining matches and make up the six goal shortfall in goals scored. If that seemed unlikely, Lions fans were starting to feel anything could go against them. Watford almost proved this with a stunning 6-3 win over Grimsby to give themselves hope of avoiding the drop after they had appeared doomed weeks before.

Stoke arrived at The Den for Millwall's penultimate match of the season with promotion ambitions; elsewhere, eyes would be on Fratton Park, Elm Park and Roots Hall:

Portsmouth v Ipswich
Reading v Sheffield United
Southend v Oldham

After an understandably nervy start, Millwall started to press for that all-important first goal in over three hours of football. Instead it was Stoke that caught Millwall with the old one-two just after the half hour mark when strikes from Sheeran and Sturridge in the space of four minutes had The

Lions well and truly on the ropes.

The second half provided Millwall with little relief and a Sturridge penalty in the 71st minute signalled game over - although most fans in the stadium had sensed that from the moment Stoke had taken the lead.

Two goals from Alex Rae in the final ten minutes should have set up a grandstand finish for an unlikely point that could have proved crucial in the fight for survival but the fiery Scottish midfielder signed off on his season - and his Millwall career - in the bleakest possible way.

The atmosphere around The Den as fans made their way home was positively funereal. News reaching them that both Pompey and Reading had lost at home was of very little consolation because now Millwall would travel to Ipswich for the final match of the season knowing that defeat could inexplicably send them down.

Elsewhere Oldham had nicked another precious point and along with Reading would play their game in hand three days later. The only consolation being it was at home to the same Stoke side that had beaten The Lions in their quest for promotion. Reading were also at home - to a Wolves side who were themselves perilously close to the drop zone but probably safe.

Based on how Millwall's season had unravelled since nervously holding on to their league top spot with a home win over Ipswich back in November there was little surprise to hear that Oldham and Reading had managed to win their crucial games in hand to ease past Millwall in the table and make that return match with Ipswich on the final day one of the most important in almost fifteen years for Millwall Football Club.

Final matches to be played May 5th 1996:
Birmingham v Reading
Ipswich v Millwall

Huddersfield v Portsmouth
Watford v Leicester

With Huddersfield and Birmingham having nothing to play for, and Ipswich able to nick the final play-off place with a win having a superior goal average, Millwall were arguably facing the toughest task and despite Watford facing play-off chasing Leicester, they were also within reach so The Lions were looking over their shoulder at not one but two teams. With their vastly inferior goal average, Pompey could overhaul them with a win meaning a draw at Ipswich would not be enough so Millwall *had* to go all out.

Endsleigh League Division One - April 27th 1996							
	P	W	D	L	F	A	PTS
19. Reading	45	12	17	16	52	62	53
20. Oldham	45	13	14	18	52	50	53
21. MILLWALL	**45**	**13**	**12**	**20**	**43**	**63**	**51**
22. Portsmouth	45	12	13	20	60	69	49
23. Watford	45	10	18	17	62	69	48
24. Luton	45	11	12	22	40	63	45

11

Wall comes tumbling down

May 1996...
Glenn Hoddle to take over from Terry Venables as
England coach after Euro 96;
Manchester United clinch Premier League title
over Keegan's Newcastle then become first team to
win the double twice when they beat Liverpool in
the FA Cup Final;
The Tories are trounced in local elections as
Tony Blair's Labour Party continue to grow in
popularity;

From 3pm on Saturday August 12th, 1995 in south London until 3:08pm on Sunday May 5th 1996 in Ipswich, Millwall had never entered the relegation places of the First Division. A journey that had begun in bright, late summer sunshine, full of excitement, optimism and expectation of a promotion season to add to the colourful history of the club, ended 200 miles away when a former player from their First Division glory days crossed the ball for Portsmouth to score - and drop Millwall into the relegation places.

Hudddersfield had nothing to play for. Ipswich meanwhile were desperate for a win that would see them beat Leicester to a place in the play-offs. Millwall knew that a win would be enough to guarantee them survival - just months after leading the table. Neither The Lions or Pompey were form horses going into that fateful final day - but that's why they were fighting for their lives.

A run of just two wins in their previous 14 matches had seen Terry Fenwick's side drop from eleventh to 22nd, Millwall meanwhile had an even less impressive ratio of two victories from their previous 18, dating back to a 1-1 Den draw with Portsmouth way back in January when they were still occupying the final play-off place. On that occasion it was Burton who struck to deny Millwall all three points with a 74th minute equaliser to cancel out Jason Van Blerk's first half opener. Not only would that Deon Burton goal contribute to Millwall's eventual fate, but he would score again on the final day to seal it.

The last time Millwall had gone into the final match of the season needing a win to survive was thirteen years earlier. George Graham had arrived mid-season with the club in one of its now familiar periods of crisis. Peter Anderson's woeful team of misfits and expensive has-beens had seen the club staring Fourth Division football in the face for the first time in almost thirty years. Despite a gallant effort to completely overhaul the side, ride out - to the disbelief of the long-suffering fans - an initial dip in results, and string together a run to claw themselves to safety, Graham's Lions had seemed to run out of games. They went into the final fixture of the 1982-83 season needing a win at Chesterfield to stay up but in the sort of form that usually accompanies promotion pushes: just one defeat in their previous twelve which was away to champions-elect Oxford.

A Dave Cusack penalty was enough to seal a 1-0 win and with results elsewhere going in their favour, safety. In fact, as it turned out, a 0-0 draw would have been enough. It would have left The Lions on 53 points - the same as Reading who occupied the final relegation place - but Millwall would have ousted The Royals by the slenderest of margins - by having a better goal difference. By one.

The fickle finger of footballing fate often plays such tricks, and you can sometimes see symmetry unfold through the years as teams go up one season and down the next. So it was to be that, while the planets truly aligned to help Millwall survive on that May day in 1983 - which in turn led to the club slowly climbing the leagues and eventually reach their long-awaited Nirvana of The First Division just five years later, it would transpire that May 5th 1996 would be the day Millwall returned to English football's third tier - in the cruellest possible way.

The nerves which contributed to Ipswich's ultimately unsuccessful play-off bid, coupled with similar stage fright from a Millwall team that had barely tasted victory all year and yet needed a win to survive, led to stalemate. From the moment ex Lions winger Jimmy Carter crossed for Burton to fire Portsmouth into a ninth-minute lead, their result was never in any doubt and 'keeper Knight barely troubled. When the full time whistles sounded at both Huddersfield's McAlpine Stadium and Ipswich's Portman Road, the emotions both on and off the pitch couldn't have been more contrasting.

As Pompey partied, both Millwall's players and fans entered a surreal world where they struggled to come to terms with what the results meant. The Lions, with 52 points, had been relegated. Weeks after surpassing what they believed was the 'safety point' of 50 points, they were down. It was that most hollow of feelings in football where, finally, there are no more chances. No more midweek matches to look towards to try and claw the points back and climb out of danger. That was it. All over. Millwall were down. Since three points for a win had been introduced back in 1981, no team had been relegated from the Second Division with 52 points. The safety line had certainly risen after the division was increased from 22 to 24 teams in

1988-89, but only Birmingham in 1993-94 had amassed more than 49 points and found themselves relegated. It was against Birmingham a month earlier that a 2-0 win had seen Millwall reach that same total of 51 points and spark celebrations at the final whistle believing it to be enough. With four games still to play, it should have been. Even in the stinking form The Lions found themselves in.

And so once more football taught us to take nothing for granted. It wouldn't matter which direction the finger of blame would point over the agonising months of the close-season as The Lions' fans pondered trips to York, Wrexham and Plymouth instead of Arsenal, West Ham and Spurs. The final table, as always, had the last word.

Endsleigh League Division One Final Table 1995-96

	Team	Pld	W	D	L	GF	GA	GD	Pts
1	Sunderland	46	22	17	7	59	33	+26	83
2	Derby County	46	21	16	9	71	51	+20	79
3	Crystal Palace	46	20	15	11	67	48	+19	75
4	Stoke City	46	20	13	13	60	49	+11	73
5	Leicester City	46	19	14	13	66	60	+6	71
6	Charlton Athletic	46	17	20	9	57	45	+12	71
7	Ipswich Town	46	19	12	15	79	69	+10	69
8	Huddersfield Town	46	17	12	17	61	58	+3	63
9	Sheffield United	46	16	14	16	57	54	+3	62
10	Barnsley	46	14	18	14	60	66	−6	60
11	WBA	46	16	12	18	60	68	−8	60
12	Port Vale	46	15	15	16	59	66	−7	60
13	Tranmere Rovers	46	14	17	15	64	60	+4	59
14	Southend United	46	15	14	17	52	61	−9	59
15	Birmingham City	46	15	13	18	61	64	−3	58
16	Norwich City	46	14	15	17	59	55	+4	57
17	Grimsby Town	46	14	14	18	55	69	−14	56
18	Oldham Athletic	46	14	14	18	54	50	+4	56
19	Reading	46	13	17	16	54	63	−9	56
20	Wolves	46	13	16	17	56	62	−6	55
21	Portsmouth	46	13	13	20	61	69	−8	52
22	Millwall	46	13	13	20	43	63	−20	52
23	Watford	46	10	18	18	62	70	−8	48
24	Luton Town	46	11	12	23	40	64	−24	45

96/97

shock, doc,
& two
smoking
barrels

SOuth Bermondsey homesick Blues

12

heRe we go agaIn

June 1996...
England host the 1996 European Championships
which are won by Germany who defeat The Czech
Republic in the final after defeating Terry
Venables' England in the semi-final on penalties;
Chelsea sign French defender Frank Leboeuf for a
club record £2.5million;
The IRA plant the UK mainland's biggest bomb
since World War Two outside a Manchester shopping
centre...
July 1996...
The FA reveal they are to bid to host the 2006
World Cup in England;
Middlesbrough sign Fabrizio Ravanelli for
£7million;
The Spice Girls' debut single Wannabe is released;
South African President Nelson Mandela visits the
UK...

Change following relegation was fleeting and widespread at The Den. The expected exodus of quality players began when Alex Rae secured the Premier League place that no Millwall fan could rightfully deny him with a move to newly-crowned First Division champions Sunderland. In his six seasons at the club he had established himself as one of the finest midfielders the club had seen. Regularly posting double figure goal totals each season, he left with a stunning Millwall career total of 71 goals - easily in the club's all-time top ten, far and away the best totals for a midfielder and a statistic that may never be beaten.

Young defender Ben Thatcher made the now familiar short trip for the pick of Millwall's young talent to Wimbledon. The Dons' side was by now resembling something akin to what is shown to the losers on television darts game show Bullseye. With Joe Kinnear's team thriving in the top flight, Thatcher joined Kenny Cunningham and Jon Goodman, showing Millwall fans what they could've done had the club been able to keep them rather than cash in and spend the money on an ultimately failed gamble to win promotion to the top flight by bringing in expensive players from elsewhere. Opinion was split among Lions fans as to whether the changes should have extended to the manager. Most felt Jimmy Nicholl could not possibly be blamed for the dramatic fall from grace which had arguably started while Mick McCarthy was still at the helm. Others feared he was out of his depth in the cut-throat world of the English League whether it be at the second or third tier. Chairman Peter Mead remained loyal to Nicholl however, even providing him with funds to rebuild. The change of manager would soon be taken out of everyone's hands though.

There was little evidence of the storm clouds that were slowly but surely gathering over the still gleaming new stands at The Den as pre-season plans began to be laid. New stands that would host, almost laughably, Third Division football. It may have been rebranded The Second Division but Millwall fans knew that they would be watching third tier fare and the likes of Gillingham and York for the first time in over a decade.

Millwall at this level was hardly something new, they had spent the majority of their Football League history in the Third Division. Spells in Division Two in the late sixties and early seventies soon gave way to Division Three once more in 1975 and again in 1979 and it was widely accepted by The Lions' long-suffering fans. Even when the struggle continued in the early eighties, this gave way to an brief but remarkable era when promotion to the First Division was finally achieved in 1988.

Now that Millwall fans had a taste of that, being back where they were in those dark days of 1980 to 1985 was hard to take. While one of the stars of that promotion side Teddy Sheringham had continued his ascent through the game as one of England's stand out performers at *Euro '96*, Lions fans were left to once again wonder what could have been.

Another reminder of Millwall's downgraded status was their new sponsor. Captain Morgan had, unsurprisingly, decided not to extend what had been a tempestuous relationship with the club where their investment had overseen a play-off riot and a shock relegation. Millwall now turned to the local newspaper for support and The South London Press were happy to be emblazoned across the much more low-key home shirt for the new season.

The usually anticipated fixtures announcement was viewed through the reluctant fingers of Millwall supporters. They must have winced to see a home season opener against Wrexham. A trip to Watford to face a fellow relegation side would be followed by York away. That was probably enough in itself to remind Lions fans that no, it hadn't all been a bad dream.

Before that there was a pre-season tour of Scotland and a visit from Liverpool - a match agreed as part of the deal that took Mark Kennedy to Anfield two years earlier.

The jaunt north of the border was of course partly down to their manager's old stomping ground and replaced McCarthy's favoured Irish tour of previous seasons. The Scottish connection, which dated back to Millwall's very roots and some of their founding fathers, the choice of colours and club emblem was continued with four new Jimmy Nicholl signings: Dave Sinclair, Jason Dair, Paul Hartley and Steve Crawford.

Sinclair, Dair and Crawford were reunited with their old boss, joining from Nicholl's previous club Raith Rovers. Sinclair was heralded as something of an enforcer - with some risky comparisons being made with a certain Terry Hurlock, something that would be closely scrutinised by the hyper-critical Millwall faithful. After winning the Scottish League Cup with Nicholl at Raith, the boss was quoted as saying: *"Even Davie Sinclair was crying and he's so tough he's got tattoos on his teeth."*

Little was known of any of the new recruits, Dair a midfielder and Crawford who played in attack but with the addition of Hartley, a winger from Hamilton Academical, the club had brought in what fans could only hope was a new spine of a side that would find the English League third tier no more of a challenge than the Scottish top flight. All four made their debuts in the first match of the Scottish tour at the end of July when Nicholl's men faced Ayr United. With goalkeeper Kasey Keller about to sign on the dotted line for newly promoted Premier League Leicester in a deal for just shy of £1million (a transaction which no doubt allowed the arrival of the four Scottish imports) Tim Carter took his place between the sticks behind a fairly familiar defence of Newman, Van Blerk, Stevens and new boy Sinclair.

The experienced back line inexplicably crumpled in the face of a team also about to start their league campaign in the third tier and a 3-0 half time deficit quickly became 4-0 just after the break. A shell-shocked Nicholl rang the changes shortly after Crawford scrambled home his first goal for the club on the hour mark, changing from 4-4-2 to 3-5-2 but Ayr continued to dominate and let The Lions off the hook when they hit the bar with a penalty after a Van Blerk handball. If Nicholl could take any positives from the game it would have been the quickly blossoming partnership of Malkin and Crawford. The ex-Tranmere front man who had been one of the few consistent performers in Millwall's disastrous previous season was complementing the Scottish striker well, setting up his first, winning the penalty for a second and helping on Newman's corner to give Crawford a debut hat-trick leaving a slightly less alarming 4-3 scoreline to the defeat.

Another third tier side awaited four days later in Stranraer and another of Millwall's new recruits scored his first goal for the club. Hartley finished off a slick move in the 20th minute between Savage and Malkin. Crawford was on target again to make it 2-0 and Malkin got a thoroughly deserved first goal of the tour to make it 3-0 just before half time.

The Lions survived the second penalty in two games when once again the spot kick rebounded to safety from the bar shortly after the hosts had got themselves back into the game to make it 3-1. But it was Hartley who stole the show this time with a glorious curling effort to put the seal on a much better performance and a 4-1 win to take to the third and final game at Premier Division Kilmarnock.

Nicholl started with a 5-4-1 line-up and it proved as disastrous as the first match, Millwall finding themselves 3-0 behind before half time. A rethink to 4-4-2 saw a better display after the break and it was Hartley on target once more to reduce the arrears. Crawford then made it five goals in three starts and The Lions looked good for a stunning comeback - only for their defence to be breached with alarming ease once more to end a goal-fest of a tour with a 4-2 victory for Kilmarnock.

Jimmy Nicholl had plenty to ponder as he prepared his

side for their final pre-season match. On the plus side, his team looked to have the sort of attacking power so sadly lacking the previous season. Malkin and Crawford had acquired an almost instant telepathy that is vital for striking partnerships and the ex-Raith hitman certainly knew where the goal was. The jury was still out on Dair and pretender to Hurlock's throne Sinclair, but Hartley looked to have all the hallmarks of what Millwall fans loved to see: pacey, tricky wingplay with an eye for goal.

The downside was of course his defence had shipped nine goals in three matches and even more alarming was the way they found themselves 3-0 behind before half time. True Nicholl was still experimenting with defensive and general team line-up permutations, but with just one match against Premier League title-hopefuls Liverpool left before the season's curtain-raiser at home to Wrexham, it was a puzzle he had to find a solution for quickly.

Ayr would go on to win promotion from the Scottish Second Division while Stranraer would have a season of struggle at the same level. Kilmarnock would survive in the Scottish top flight. The early scrutiny of Millwall's promotion credentials from what would be a very tough English Second Division did not bode well. Even a goalless draw with a strong Liverpool side containing David James, Mark Wright, Michael Thomas, Stan Collymore, Robbie Fowler, John Barnes, Steve McManaman and ex-Lions Phil Babb and Neil Ruddock in front of a healthy crowd of over 14,000 did little to convince those present that promotion would be easy to win. They'd already made that mistake twelve months earlier. Each game would be a battle. Millwall would be seen as the big fish now, there to be shot at and most of the Second Division clubs would be relishing a trip to the impressive new Den much more than the old place. So many factors were against Nicholl's side. For all the promise his new signings showed, neither they, nor many of the squad he had inherited had experience at this level, which, in the dog-eat-dog world of the English league third tier, can often spell struggle.

There was no other way around it, Millwall had to hit the ground running, fix their defensive shortcomings, pick up where they left off with their attacking prowess on the Scottish tour and start with a win against Wrexham.

13

goals from Newcastle...

August 1996...
Entrepreneur Chris Wright buys QPR for £10m;
Bruce Grobelaar faces court over match-fixing
allegations;
Arsenal sack Bruce Rioch after 61 weeks in charge;
The Prince and Princess of Wales complete their
divorce proceedings after fifteen years of
marriage...

An encouraging Den crowd of just under 10,000 turned up to see Millwall start a season in English football's third tier for the first time since 1984. Back then, less than half that attendance had seen Millwall easily brush aside Swansea 2-0 in what was to be the first step towards promotion. This time another team from across the Welsh border were the visitors but Jimmy Nicholl's new-look Lions found Wrexham a far tougher proposition and by the end of the match, very few of the Millwall supporters that had witnessed an uninspiring 1-1 draw with Brian Flynn's side felt they had witnessed the start of a climb back into Division One.

In fact, were it not for Steve Crawford's penalty eight minutes from time, the season would have started with a defeat and Wrexham, who dominated a disjointed Millwall for much of the match, could feel aggrieved they didn't head back to north Wales with all three points. Crawford's debut goal was however some cause for optimism. One thing Nicholl needed was goals, the other was to shore up the leaky defence that had shipped so many goals on that tour of Scotland and so the news that Tony Witter was back in the Millwall squad was welcomed by fans. The popular pacey central defender had fallen out of favour with Nicholl since his arrival and seemed to be at the end of his Millwall career, but a change of heart - somewhat enforced by a growing injury list - saw the fans' favourite back in the fold.

Chairman Peter Meade was typically upbeat about the new season, and took the opportunity to explain the Summer departures and arrivals (which as he was at pains to point out showed greater ambition than any of their Division Two rivals). Like his predecessor Reg Burr, he was also keen to jump to Millwall fans' defence after some typically lazy journalism during the summer's Euro 96 tournament:

"We're all looking forward to the new season now I think. Whilst we would certainly rather be playing in the First Division, I believe that there are good reasons for approaching 1996/97 with a healthy degree of optimism, and I for one am excited at the prospect of watching the likes of Steve Crawford, Jason Dair, Paul Hartley and Davey Sinclair. This week of course Kasey Keller left us, and in truth we always rather expected this to happen any time as a result of the Bosman ruling, which means that at the end of this season he would have been a free agent and able to return to the States or play abroad effectively on a free transfer. Having established himself in the American team, we were aware that he felt he needed to play at a higher level in order to maintain that position. Under the terms of his contract, we had to inform Kasey of any enquiries that were made for him, so it was almost inevitable that he would be leaving us sooner or later, and for the reason outlined above relating to Bosman, the best result for Millwall has been achieved by Kasey joining Leicester

this week. Initially Leicester made us an offer of £600,000 which I wasn't prepared to entertain, believing that even with less than a year on his contract remaining Kasey was worth getting on for a million of anybody's money.

In the end the figure we received was just short of that, and I felt that we had done a reasonable deal given that in under twelve months time I'm convinced we'd have had to give him away for nothing. He was also one of the biggest wage earners at the club so all round this deal made sound financial sense. Naturally, just as with Alex and Ben there is a sadness in seeing Kasey leave. He has given us five years good service and become a real favourite at The Den. We wish him all the very best for his future in the Premiership. I think at the same time, we have to remember that whilst we have sold some players in the summer, no-one in our division has got close to the sort of purchases we have made. We are taking the coming season very seriously and the early indications are very good indeed. I was delighted with almost everything about the evening when we played Liverpool, although I do apologise to anyone who had difficulty getting in. We are having another look at our ticketing system to see if we can do that any better. Most important was the impeccable behaviour of everyone.

This week we had eleven people arrested at a cricket match and two hundred ejected. If that had happened here we'd have attracted banner headlines, so it does just re-emphasise the need for us to maintain our standards because certain elements in the media are always on the lookout for a nice Millwall/hooligan story. In that respect, let me just say that we have conducted a full investigation into allegations which appeared in The Mail suggesting that Millwall fans were at the forefront of the trouble which occurred during EURO '96 after the England v Germany game and have found no evidence to support that view. We will be making our findings fully available to the newspaper concerned, but I daresay we won't receive anywhere near the same coverage under a 'Millwall fans not to blame' heading."

There was more encouraging signs four days later when Crawford's strike partner Chris Malkin opened his account for the season and a Witter-inspired defence kept its first clean sheet in a 1-0 League Cup first round first leg victory over Peterborough. Things improved further on Millwall's first away trip of the season to a Watford side that were, like Millwall, aiming to bounce straight back into Division One. Goals either side of half time from Michael Harle and Crawford again were enough to give Nicholl a rare taste of victory, another defensive shut-out and an early place in the top six. The first goal was particularly pleasing for Harle who had become something of a forgotten man since he joined with Neil Emblen from Sittingbourne three years earlier. While Emblen had gone straight into Millwall's side and earned himself a move to Wolves, full-back Harle had found himself unable to break into the first team until the departure of Ben Thatcher and injury to Jason Van Blerk saw him finally make his Lions debut at Vicarage Road - and mark it with a goal.

Things seemed to be going even better three days later when they travelled to bottom-of-the-table York and raced into a 2-0 half time lead thanks to goals from Savage and Malkin. But it didn't take long for the old bad habits to reappear in the second half as soon as the hosts pulled a goal back from the penalty spot. Twenty minutes after that spot-kick award, Millwall found themselves 3-2 behind and slipping to their first defeat of the season.

Fortunately Millwall were able to round off the month by returning to winning ways in a 2-1 win at home to Burnley. A mad nine minute spell saw The Lions take the lead through Ricky Newman in the 70th minute, relinquish it to a Nogan equaliser just five minutes later then clinch the points thanks to Lucas Neill. It was enough to see them leapfrog Burnley into the top six but another decent 9,000 Den crowd were still less than convinced of their team's promotion credentials in what was already looking to be a very open division with no stand-out contenders for the top places.

Any team that could find some consistency would be able to open up a useful early lead at the top of the table, but whilst Millwall had looked good in patches so far, they had also shown worrying signs of the same brittle defensive lapses that had cost them their place in Division One. To make matters worse, Nicholl's injury list was starting to pile up, leading him to lament:

"In all the clubs I've been at as a player an manager I can't remember an injury list like this at this stage of the season."

Far more pressing than putting together a string of wins to challenge at the top of the table was the basic task of picking 14 fit footballers to take to the field for the next match.

Just five matches into the new season, Millwall were already running out of players and in need of new blood. Fortunately it arrived, and made an instant impact.

September 1996...
New England manager Glenn Hoddle gets off to a winning start with a 3-0 World Cup 98 qualifying win over Moldova;
Leeds sack manager Howard Wilkinson four years after he led them to the League title and replace him with ex-Arsenal manager George Graham;
Ray Wilkins shocks QPR fans by resigning as manager; Ford launches its new Ka model...

September began with the short trip to Peterborough for the second leg of Millwall's League Cup first round tie where they were to be haunted by a familiar face from their recent past. Striker Ken Charlery had blossomed right on

Millwall's doorstep at Fisher Athletic and had gone on to score regularly at several other clubs. Now in his third spell at Peterborough, he'd made the move from Birmingham in the summer, where one of his last goals for the midlands side had been the last minute equaliser in the 2-2 draw with Millwall when both sides were battling it out for the First Division top spot just ten months earlier.

Fifteen minutes into the match it was Charlery again on target to net his 100th career goal and level the tie on aggregate. With the match heading for an extra thirty minutes that Nicholl's threadbare squad could well do without, salvation seemed to arrive in the shape of a late penalty award for The Lions - only for Jason Dair to see his spot kick saved. Extra time saw more stalemate until Griffiths put Millwall out of their misery with the decider six minutes from time.

Absent from that defeat were Dave Savage and Steve Crawford. The Irish midfielder had suffered medial knee ligament damage and his experience and ability to pop up with the odd vital goal would be sorely missed. Crawford was nursing a less serious ankle knock but when his strike partner left the Peterborough pitch with a severely swollen ankle and mild concussion, suddenly Nicholl's goalscoring options were frighteningly limited going into the next league game at home to Ian Holloway's Bristol Rovers four days later with neither striker being fit enough to start the match. Fortunately, salvation was on the way - from Newcastle.

Darren Huckerby was an unknown name to the Millwall faithful who took their seats at The Den for the next match against Bristol Rovers. The last time the two sides had met had been for the emotional farewell to the old Den when an already relegated Rovers crashed the party with a 3-0 win. Huckerby had caught the eye of Newcastle scouts when he broke into the Lincoln City first team and scored five goals in his debut season. But with Kevin Keegan's side challenging for the Premier League title the young striker's opportunities had been understandably limited - and quickly became Millwall's gain.

It took him just an hour to show Millwall fans what he was capable of, rounding off an impressive display of strength and skill with a debut goal to seal a 2-0 win and push The Lions into the top four going into another trip to Peterborough three days later - this time for a league encounter.

A similarly cagey first half to the League Cup clash seven days before saw Posh go into the half time break 1-0 up but the second half was about to explode into action and produce more incident in 45 minutes than the previous 255 between the two sides had.

Huckerby was on target again soon after the restart to level the match only for that man Charlery yet again to haunt The Lions with another goal and give his side the lead. Lucas Neill pulled Millwall level once more but the match appeared to be settled five minutes from time when a goal from O'Connor put Peterborough 3-2 ahead. Then, with injury time ticking down, up popped a fit-again Chris Malkin to snatch a last gasp leveller.

Whilst team spirit appeared healthy on the surface, a comment by Nicholl in his programme notes before that Bristol Rovers victory had a few fans wondering if all was as it should be in the dressing room. Talking about Jason Dair's spot kick miss in the cup tie at Peterborough, he somewhat cryptically explained:

"...I think it summed it all up when we got the penalty near the end and the keeper made a good save from Jason Dair's kick. I felt sorry for Jason and I made one or two points after the game which I don't want to go over again."

It seemed an odd comment to make without further

explanation and may well have had nothing to do with the harmony in the dressing room where fallouts often occur immediately after a defeat and are quickly resolved but nevertheless it was some small cause for concern for the fans reading it who were only too aware of their side's paper-thin resilience at that time.

Huckerby's influence continued to show in a 2-1 win away to Notts County where, whilst he didn't score, he showed a class and quality that was way above anything Division Two had to offer and whilst one player doesn't make a team, in a very ordinary league a Darren Huckerby was exactly what was required to give Millwall that edge over their promotion rivals and a quick route back up.

With Huckerby already looking like part of the furniture and on target again in the next match at home to Crewe - his third goal in four matches - talk obviously started about Millwall's prospects of signing him permanently.

As is often the case, the rumour mill was in full swing with varying stories circulating that ranged from Newcastle being pleased with Huckerby's progress and keen to get him into The Magpies' first team, to them being willing to let him go if the price was right. That was of course the major fly in the ointment: money. Chairman Peter Mead had already explained the cost-cutting measures that club had to undertake following relegation, but had also made it clear that a sizeable chunk of funds had been made available to Nicholl to bring in new players.

Promotion to Division One didn't bring the boost in finances that getting into the Premier League did, so it was hard to underwrite a big money signing for a Division Two promotion push. But, with talk of Newcastle wanting £1million for the young striker, Millwall fans celebrating a late winner at Notts County were wondering if the club were, as the rumours now suggested, about to break their transfer record to sign a major piece in their promotion jigsaw. These rumours were given more substance when, in his programme notes before the match with Crewe, Jimmy Nicholl tantalised fans with what seemed to be a statement of intent to make the loan signing of Huckerby a permanent one:

"...I hope he finishes his loan period with another couple of goals and I'll certainly be looking to do something after that."

Quite what that 'something' was, fans were unaware but, with the loan system being much more rigid and restrictive back in 1996, Huckerby's spell would have to end on October 5th with either him returning to Tyneside, or becoming a Millwall player.

His latest contribution in a 2-0 win over Crewe had seen Millwall jump into second spot - an automatic promotion place. Huckerby's brief influence had transformed Millwall from a side taking one step forwards and one back in search of a play-off berth to a team that looked every bit champions-in-waiting. Millwall simply *had* to do that deal.

14

it's the hope that kills you

October 1996...
Manchester City name Steve Coppell as their new
manager;
Chelsea director Matthew Harding dies in a
helicopter crash;
A double car bomb attack by the IRA at the Thiepval
British Army HQ kills one soldier and injures 31
others;
The Conservative government's majority is reduced
to just one after the defection of Peter Thurnham
to the Liberal Democrats...

Darren Huckerby's last loan appearance for
Millwall wouldn't be - as it should have been -
the away trip to Plymouth Argyle on October 5th.
He played probably his most unproductive 90 minutes of
his brief Millwall career so far in a hugely disappointing
2-1 defeat away to struggling Preston and then made
his final bow in a mad 90 minutes at home to Stockport
County - where, as far as his future as a Millwall player
was concerned, confusion reigned.

Huckerby graced the cover of he programme for the
midweek Den clash with County and Jimmy Nicholl was
at pains to explain in his programme notes the lengths he
had gone to in order to persuade Newcastle boss Kevin

Keegan to at least let him extend his loan period for another two months. Despite hints to the contrary from the Millwall chairman, all talk of a permanent move for the striker seemed to be now off the table. Of course, with the vagaries of printing deadlines, Nicholl's notes were penned before the latest edition of The South London Press had published it's Tuesday edition - 24 hours before the visit of Dave Jones' County to SE16 - by which time the hopes of signing Huckerby even for a further two matches let alone two months had been crushed.

Despite only making one appearance since his £400,000 move to St James Park from Lincoln, Newcastle boss Kevin Keegan was insisting that Huckerby was now an important part of his squad with commitments from both the Premier League and European schedules building up and rumours that Colombian striker Faustino Asprilla was unhappy.

"Darren's coming back once his loan period is up" Keegan explained. "I know Jimmy wanted to keep him but we need him here".

Such is the dangers of the loan system for a lower league club. If it works out, it's great, but then the impact of not being able to make that move permanent can have a disastrous effect on team morale. If it doesn't work out, a club on a tight budget has saved itself from losing vital funds in an expensive gamble of a permanent signing. Typically in this case, Millwall were to come off worse from what started out as a highly successful loan signing - and not for the first time either. Of course, often a club will want to loan a player out purely to give him much needed experience with no desire to let him leave on a permanent basis - although on this occasion, whilst nothing was officially placed on record, there were murmurings emanating from Newcastle that they were happy to let him go and make a quick half a million pounds profit so the sudden change of heart by

Keegan appeared strange.

Huckerby made what would prove to be his last ever appearance in a Millwall shirt in a frenetic seven goal thriller with Stockport but for the second successive match did not get on the scoresheet. Instead, despite two quick goals from Rogan and Hartley clawing The Lions back from 1-3 down to 3-3 with twenty minutes left, Armstrong scored a last minute winner for the visitors to inflict Millwall's fist home defeat of the season and send them back down to sixth place in the table. Just a few weeks later, Huckerby would sign for Premier League Coventry for a reported fee of £1million and score his first goal for the club in a 2-1 win - over Newcastle.

For Jimmy Nicholl and Millwall, it was back to the drawing board.

Far from wallow in self pity however, Millwall shrugged off the disappointment of losing Huckerby with a spirited 0-0 draw at Plymouth where, were it not for another penalty miss, they could have taken all three points. Back at The Den they showed plenty of spirit after falling behind to Chesterfield to grab two quick goals before half time and this time another missed penalty didn't prevent them from taking all three points and set them off on an unbeaten run which would last the whole month. Second placed Bury were next to visit The Den and were beaten 1-0 thanks to another goal from Anton Rogan. The veteran defender was enjoying something of a goalscoring spree with that strike making it four goals in three matches.

Steve Crawford, who had been forced to play a wide role following the success of Huckerby and Malkin's partnership, was now back in his familiar striker's role (with Malkin leaving to join Blackpool) and grabbed two goals in another win - 3-2 at Gillingham - which set The Lions up perfectly in second place for the trip to top-of-the-table Brentford. A hard-earned 0-0 draw at Griffin Park was made all the more satisfying four days later when they wrapped up the month with a record of four wins and two draws as Blackpool were beaten 2-1 - despite taking a first half lead through, somewhat inevitably, Chris Malkin. Anton Rogan's goalscoring prowess continued and was enhanced by him becoming The Lions' new penalty taker which he took full advantage of by scoring twice from the spot to complete the comeback win over The Tangerines.

Rather than fall to pieces following the departure of Darren Huckerby, Millwall had been galvanised and - although somewhat quietly and unspectacularly - had eased themselves into contention for a top two place. That said, despite Millwall's outwardly looking rude health, cracks were beginning to show and storm clouds were very gradually gathering.

November 1996...
Steve Coppell leaves his post as manager of Manchester City after just 33 days in the job;
Wales are beaten 7-1 by Holland in a World Cup qualifier;
Terry Venables becomes coach of the Australian national team;
Labour lead The Conservatives by 17 points in the latest polls just six months before the next general election;
The Channel Tunnel is closed when a truck on a transporter wagon catches fire...

The relationship between Millwall fans and the players and management has often been a delicate one. It can be ticking along fine but the merest of incidents can damage it immediately - and irreparably. With sensitivities already running high following on from the bitter disappointment of the previous season's demise and the faltering start to the new season, many Millwall fans were still not convinced of either Nicholl's managerial credentials or his side's promotion prospects.

There was a glimpse of just how close to braking point they were when, following that dramatic late defeat at home to Stockport, an irate Lions fan stormed onto the visitors' team coach as it was preparing to leave and head back to the north west. The fuming supporter had apparently been having a regular exchange with the Stockport winger throughout the eventful second half and, following County's late victory the player had seemingly decided to have the last word as he disappeared down the tunnel. The fan had other ideas and demanded to be introduced to the player so he could continue the row, fortunately, the diplomatic skills of the visitors' commercial manager quelled the situation.

Rucking with the opposition is one thing, but once the arguing starts amongst your own, the problems really begin and the first signs of unravelling were apparent - if only in the smallest possible way at the next home match with Chesterfield. A mistake by Bobby Bowry led to Chris Beaumont giving the visiting Spireites the lead and from that moment, every time Bowry came near the ball - or the home fans - he was roundly booed. Nicholl understandably took exception to this and had several frank discussions about it with some of the perpetrators in the West Stand behind his dugout but he then used his programme notes in the next match against Bury to voice his concerns about the incident. It won't have been the first time fans and manager have not seen eye to eye but once the matter was set out in print, many Millwall fans will have seen that as lines being drawn, lines that would prove to be indelible.

The best way to paper over footballing cracks is of course to win matches and reach the top of the league - which is precisely what Millwall did in their next home match against Walsall. An early goal from Crawford in front of another 9,000 crowd was enough to send Millwall to the top of the table. However, coming as it did almost exactly a year to the day since they had gone top of the First Division, not a single Lions fan in that crowd was getting carried away. Crawford's rich form continued with another goal in the 1-1 draw away to Bristol City as The Lions retained top spot and extended their unbeaten run to eight since departure of the talismanic Huckerby.

Another great footballing tonic is a cup run and, after their early exit in the League Cup hopes were high of an FA Cup adventure. As a third tier team once more, Millwall found themselves in FA Cup action from the first round stage and the draw handed them a tricky trip to Woking. The Conference side had a giantkilling reputation and the live TV cameras were present in the hope of witnessing a shock, which looked likely when the home side took a fourth minute lead but goals from Crawford and Savage turned the match in Millwall's favour before the break.

Since the second half debacle against Stockport, Millwall had only conceded more than one goal on one occasion and a defensive rigidity was finally starting to show which was instrumental in taking them to the top of the table, unfortunately they were still prone to the occasional self-destruct and that was in evidence once more as Woking were allowed back in the tie with a second half penalty which veteran Clive Walker gratefully despatched to earn his side a replay at The Den.

Fortunately Crawford was on target again in the next league match with both goals in a 2-1 win at home to Shrewsbury and the defence was back to its miserly best in a hard-fought if not a little disappointing goalless draw at struggling Rotherham to set up another live FA Cup tie with Woking.

The Sky TV cameras were finally given the cup shock story they wanted when an alarmingly lack lustre Lions side were dumped out of the cup thanks to a single goal

from 39-year-old ex-Chelsea star Walker leaving Nicholl
with the unwelcome record of having been despatched
from both domestic cup competitions at the first stage in
his first attempts as Millwall manager.

Suddenly Millwall's goalscoring ability had deserted
them. A third successive blank was posted in the next
home league game at The Den against title rivals Brentford
although at least they weren't conceding and the 0-0 draw
with The Bees kept them on top of the table, three points
clear of the Griffin Park club going into December.

December 1996...
Blackburn announce Sven Goran Eriksson will be
their new manager in June;
Bristol Rovers players are hurt after a pitch
invasion by Bristol City fans following Rovers'
late equaliser in the derby at Ashton gate;
Sir John Gorst, 68-year-old Conservative MP for
Hendon North in London, resigns the party whip,
leaving the Conservative Party without a majority
in the House of Commons;

December was a crucial month for Millwall's promotion
push. They would face three teams in the relegation places
and Luton - who were just behind them in third. A repeat
of October's fine form would see The Lions go into the
New Year in a strong position with daylight between them
at the top of the Second Division table and the rest of what
was proving to be a very ordinary league. Unfortunately,
December was to prove more of a re-run of the disastrous
spell twelve months earlier as they once again flattered to
deceive with their position at the top of the league.

A fourth consecutive match without scoring was disappointing enough, but when bottom-of-the-table Wycombe
Wanderers scored their winner thirteen minutes from time
at Adams Park alarm bells really started to ring as Millwall
were knocked off the top spot. A 4-0 Auto Windscreens
Shield win at Hereford provided Crawford with a welcome

return to scoring as he shared the rout with Jason Dair but it failed to translate into league form as another struggling side in Bournemouth were allowed to grab a point in a 1-1 Dean Court draw.

Millwall took the lead at Bournemouth courtesy of Mark Bright, the veteran ex-Palace striker had joined The Lions to bolster their shot-shy attack and made an immediate impact but he was unable to find the net on his home debut as Luton snatched a last minute 1-0 win to leapfrog The Lions into second place.

Worse was to follow when strugglers Peterborough visited The Den on Boxing Day and eased to a 2-0 win. This had now become a recurring nightmare for Millwall's fans. A promising start, finding some form and the top of the table by November, only to fall away badly in December. The Lions were going into the New Year on the back of a six match winless league run, devoid of goals and with morale slipping almost as quickly as their league position.

But as they would soon find out, league position was the least of their problems, within weeks, Millwall Football Club would be fighting for its very existence..

15

OUr dArkest hOUr
- and a hAlf...

January 1997...
Kevin Keegan sensationally resigns as manager of
Newcastle, Barcelona manager Bobby Robson turns
down an offer to take his place and Kenny Dalglish
is installed as the new Magpies boss;
Steve Coppell returns to Crystal Palace as
part-time assistant to manager Dave Bassett;
Chris Evans resigns from the Radio 1 breakfast
show;
David Bowie performs his 50th Birthday Bash
concert (the day after his birthday) at Madison
Square Garden, New York City;
East 17 kick and member Brian Harvey out after his
public comments about Ecstasy...

If there was a glimmer of hope for Millwall's season to
receive a much needed boost, it was in the first match
of the New Year at home to Colchester in the second
round of the Auto Windscreens Shield. Here was a competition that provided teams in the third and fourth tier a
chance of a Wembley final - something that Millwall had
never experienced - at least not since their appearance in
the War Time Cup Final against Chelsea in 1944.

After comfortably disposing of Third Division Hereford
in the first round, hopes were naturally high when another
Division Three side visited The Den on a bone cold

Bermondsey winter evening and the 2,700 brave souls who assembled to see their team take another step towards a day out at Wembley were no doubt relieved to see their side lead at half time through a tenth minute Crawford goal. But from the moment flame-haired Colchester striker Tony Adcock levelled the tie early in the second half, the unravelling of Millwall's season took on a new, scary momentum.

Dave Savage restored The Lions' lead with fifteen minutes left but there was a laborious and weary nature about Millwall's play despite regaining the advantage and a certain inevitability about Adcock's last minute equaliser which sent the game into extra time. Not just the regular old extra time though, the competition had decided to experiment with the Golden Goal rule. A concept straight out of the playground, it basically meant 'next goal wins' and within 90 seconds of Millwall's first experience of he new rule they had fallen victim to it.

Millwall's team that night included two new faces - one young, the other with decades of experience. Goalkeeper Andrew Iga made the step up from the reserves to replace Tim Carter and veteran midfielder Ray Wilkins made his Millwall debut. Unfortunately neither the former inter-national playmaker - or the striking prowess of Mark Bright (who was playing the final game of his loan spell from Sheffield Wednesday) was enough to compete with the spirit of the Essex side. The final flicker of hope for Millwall's season was extinguished because, despite their league position still being healthy, the atmosphere around the club between management, players and fans had turned sickeningly toxic.

Goalkeeper Iga was abused by a small group of fans in the club car park following the Colchester defeat, something which, once again, with some justification, manager Nicholl took exception to and used his programme notes

for the next league home match against Preston to voice
his disgust. But those notes were not just a rebuke for
Millwall's fans, the players also came in for criticism in a
quite incredible rant which read like a statement of understandable exasperation - indeed, almost resignation:

*"I didn't go up to the Press conference after Tuesday
night's game because I didn't want to make excuses. I
congratulated Colchester and I didn't want to take anything
away from their performance, but I was thoroughly disappointed by how easy they found it to get in and around our
box and how easy they found it to take their goals and with
our second-half display in general.*

*I felt sorry for big Andrew Iga. It was a tough baptism
for him, but the thing that disgusted me was the personal
abuse he was subjected to in the car park afterwards. We
all have bad games and you expect criticism for it, but for
a young lad just starting out in the game, that personal
abuse will stick in his memory. As far as I'm concerned I
know I have to be thick skinned. I accept the abuse at the
moment because things haven't been going well recently.
We've been knocked out of two Cup competitions at home
by smaller clubs, and I know supporters believe that we
shouldn't be in the Second Division and that we haven't
been playing well. But I'm not just going to walk away
from the situation. I know that I wouldn't be getting this
criticism if the players were producing performances which
the supporters were happy with, not just in terms of results,
but in terms of a determination to do their utmost to try
and win games. When supporters don't see players clearly
working hard and giving their all, that's when the abuse
comes in because they will say that the manager must be
at fault because the players are not responding to him. So
what I've got to do is find players within the club who are
going to go about the job the way professional players are
expected to irrespective of whether they are confident or*

not. There's no such thing as failure, except when you don't try and it's that which gets to me sometimes. This afternoon it may well be that there will be some unfamiliar faces out there in Millwall shirts because I'm fed up with talking, and I've tried to take as much pressure off the players as I can and take the responsibility for what's happening in order to get them to relax. But I'm at the stage now where I've got to try something different and there may be players who thought they didn't have a chance of playing because they are too young or have been out of the picture who could find themselves playing against Preston. At the time of writing I'm hoping that Tim Carter will have recovered from flu in time to play, but with Jason Dair, Steve Crawford and Paul Hartley also suffering and Anton Rogan and Dave Savage taking knocks in midweek I'll have to see who's available before deciding who will play. Mark Bright's loan is up after today, so we have to decide what to do there and clearly if Mark doesn't stay with us we have to look for another striker. Towards the end of the month hopefully Tony Witter, Keith Stevens and Scott Fitzgerald will come back into things but we have to get our act together before then because there are three important games to be played this month starting this afternoon."

Nicholl had truly worn his heart on his sleeve, but that's often a bad move in football. It was clear to everyone that the club's unprecedented bad luck with injuries was hampering them, but the admission that the players at his disposal simply weren't performing for him and that his Plan B was to bring in either young previously untried players or ones that he himself had considered not up to the job in previous months painted a very foreboding picture of how life with The Lions had become.

True to his word, Nicholl gave debuts to youngsters Bircham and Roche and a return for veteran striker Richard Cadette but, in-keeping with Millwall's season, the changes papered over some cracks, and exposed new frailties. Cadette gave Millwall a 23rd-minute lead, only for Preston to respond within 60 seconds and ten minutes later were awarded a penalty which saw them go into half time 2-1 ahead and the vast majority of the 7,000 crowd growing increasingly restless. Nicholl must have been regretting his words in those programme notes when he insisted he wasn't going to just walk away, yet somehow he was able to galvanise his side at the break and within 20 minutes of the restart goals from the ever-reliable Crawford and Savage and turned the match around, giving Millwall their first league victory in nine attempts and, quite unbelievably, sent them back up to third place before their visit to Stockport who were languishing down in 17th.

What transpired in 90 horrific minutes at Edgeley Park, Stockport on January 18th, 1997 will go down in the history of Millwall Football Club as one of its darkest one and half hours. The performance and scoreline - as horrendous as it was and potentially could have been - paled into tiny insignificance when set against the news that had broke on the morning of the match: Millwall Football Club were about to go into administration.

It was probably understandable that, against this backdrop of uncertainty, where every single member of staff on the payroll at Millwall Football Club were now unsure if they'd have a job or when it would be taken from them, that on the pitch, Stockport were able to brush The Lions aside as if they were not there.

Andy Mutch gave The Hatters a twelfth-minute lead and Damien Webber's 28th minute leveller was merely a brief respite although there was an element of luck about the way Stockport were able to regain the lead three minutes later. As the ball pinged around in the Millwall box, referee Lunt pointed to the penalty spot after the ball appeared to strike Marc Bircham on the chest. Not content with this contentious decision, Lunt then showed an incredulous Bircham a red card for deliberate handball. Armstrong converted the spot kick and the match was over for The Lions. By half time County were 3-1 ahead and it was 5-1 by the 52nd minute. Mercifully, Stockport appeared to take their foot off the pedal, almost certainly saving Millwall from the biggest humiliation in their history.

The full implications of administration were not known as Millwall remained in the north west and were once again well beaten - this time 3-0 at Blackpool. In the build up to the match Millwall's shares had been suspended following pressure from creditors but, back in 1997, administration didn't carry a points penalty or quite as many far reaching implications as it does in the modern era.

That was just as well because by now, Millwall were giving away points on a weekly basis and as the details of the club's financial plight - and its road to survival - were tentatively revealed, the first small but crucial hurdle was cleared when chairman Peter Mead and two banks made the necessary investment of £850,000 to satisfy the football authorities that the club was in a position to finish the season. It was only a temporary reprieve however. After that, a buyer would need to be found and right now, buying Millwall Football Club wasn't exactly a desirable proposition. As Millwall's slide down the table - and into possible extinction continued with a 2-0 home defeat to Bristol City to end a truly depressing month for Lions fans whose patience finally snapped at the final whistle when hundreds invade the Den pitch to protest against the board and manager.

The true picture of just how bad the club's financial plight was would become clear - to a horrifying degree - in the coming weeks. Change was coming, it would be swift and far-reaching. Jimmy Nicholl knew his days at Millwall were numbered, and he was about to oversee his last match as manager, to be replaced by a very familiar face.

February 1997...
Plymouth sack manager Neil Warnock;
England lose a home World Cup match for the first
time when a Zola goal gives Italy a 1-0 win;
Terry Venables buys Portsmouth for £1;
England announce their intention to bid for the
2006 World Cup;
Moors Murderer Myra Hindley is informed by Home
Secretary Michael Howard that she will never be
released from prison;
Scientists at the Roslin Institute announce the
birth of a cloned sheep named Dolly...

Bobby Bowry gave Millwall a twelfth-minute lead at Walsall but once again The Lions' brittle resolve was soon in evidence as, just over ten minutes later they had scored the two goals required to win the match and inflict a fourth successive league defeat on Jimmy Nicholl's beleaguered side - and a seventh in nine. It was to be Nicholl's last.

On the following Monday, Millwall revealed the extent of their perilous state when they announced £1.5m of cuts at the club with 20 sackings - including manager Nicholl, the transfer-listing of twelve first team squad members and a 10% pay cut for all staff across the board. The announcement included, somewhat incongruously, the naming of a new manager who was no stranger to Millwall fans and had presided over much happier times at The Den: John Docherty.

The Doc's arrival was seen by some as a retrograde step. He had left Millwall with the side slipping out of the top flight that he had famously won them promotion to and, after an unsuccessful spell at Bradford, had been in the managerial wilderness for over six years. But in truth, Docherty was just what the club needed. After twelve months of utter turmoil, Docherty was a safe pair of hands who would be able to steady the ship, ensuring that Millwall's freefall didn't see them end up as a bottom tier club for the first time in over 30 years - and making them even harder to sell to a prospective new owner.

His first programme notes revealed an affection, passion, knowledge of the club - and more importantly the fans. Like the shrewd, time-served football man that he was, he was non-committal but unswervingly on the side of the supporters:

"The fact that I'd had a couple of journalists ring me to ask if there was any truth in a story that I would be coming back to Millwall about a week before it happened, took a little bit of the surprise element away when I eventually got a call from Peter Mead. Having such a soft spot for the club the temptation was immediately there, but I have to tell you I thought long and hard before accepting this offer. It hasn't taken long to convince me that I've done the right thing. I've had so many nice comments and well wishers that it brought a lump to my throat, and once I'd eventually got out on the training ground with the players for the first time on Wednesday I really felt I was back. I have had one or two offers in recent months including one Premier club who wanted me on the staff, but I thought no. I'm enjoying my golf and I'm not sure that I want to go back to all that. But the fact that it was now Millwall who had come in for me ultimately did make the difference. One thing I'm not blind to, however, is the fact that we've got a difficult job on here. I've got no magic wand, but just go about the job the same way I did before, work as hard as I can, encourage the players to do the same and see how we go. I don't need to ask the crowd to support us, because it goes without saying that if ever there's a crowd that supports the club it's Millwall's. They're very vociferous, hypercritical perhaps at times, but I wouldn't have it any other way. I remember when I arrived the first time, my initial thought was, 'This is just like Glasgow' The fans here were almost sucking you out of the tunnel saying "Come on, where are

you? Let us have it." Certainly the adrenalin rush that gives you was a factor in helping me decide to return. This time round, I've got David Kemp with me as my coach. I tried to sign him back in 1974 when I was at Brentford. Unfortunately I wasn't able to and he went on to score plenty of goals elsewhere. Subsequently, he's gone on to gain considerable coaching and managerial experience, including at this level. He knows what it's all about, he's keen and I'm pleased to have him here. It's great to be reunited with Bob Pearson, with whom I first worked when I held my first coaching position at QPR many years ago, and we've been together on and off ever since. If you go through the Millwall record books over the years he has been involved with this club and add up the players he has been responsible for bringing through the list is endless. We've also persuaded Keith Stevens to come onto the coaching side, although he will still continue as a player. I think you have to have a little bit of a gift if you're going to be successful on the coaching and managerial side, and I happen to think that of his type Keith will be a natural. If he wants to make a career of it he won't need to be educated. He'll work out his own way of doing things and he'll be successful at it. I was a little bit embarrassed when it was on the radio that Keith was going to be offered a coaching post before I'd even had the chance to talk to him. But like the good honest professional he is, and like the Millwall stalwart he is, his reaction was, 'Thank you very much, delighted." I hope, though, that I don't rely too much on his coaching duties just yet. I want him to recover after his operation because I still see him as an integral part of the team. A lot of managers say the only thing wrong with football is that it's great from Monday to Friday, but then something happens on, a Saturday which goes and spoils it. Whilst I've been out of the game I've certainly missed that day to day banter and camaraderie you get from working with players, but this afternoon at 3 o'clock that's what it's all about. I'm going to be leaning on Bob and Keith a little bit for a few days because I'm still getting to know everybody here, although with the injury list we've got just now I think the team will more or less pick itself today. I'm not going to make too many comments about how we're going to go about things or too many promises about how we're going to play. We have to look at building up over a period of time, getting a good solid foundation and getting back to what I consider is a team that represents Millwall's character. You can talk about systems and patterns of play, but in the end what you need is a winning formula. There's nothing better than being the supporter of a team that's winning regularly. That's what we'll be working to produce. One final comment I'd like to make: Don't always believe everything you read in newspapers, and particularly comments attributed to individuals. I've already had a player come to see me about an article which has appeared this week which has shown him up in a bad light, and he knows he didn't say some of the things which have been attributed to him. It doesn't help us, particularly at this time, if supporters believe that players are being critical when they're being nothing of the sort, so I'd just ask you to bear that in mind."

If Jimmy Nicholl had been a little caught off guard by just how passionate and vociferous Millwall's fans had been - in spite of what he must have been advised and gleaned from their well-documented reputation, The Doc was under no illusions and knew exactly how to work with them. A failing that had ultimately been Nicholl's downfall, though no fault of his own. As a Millwall manager you either get the fans or you don't. It's *never* the other way around!

If Docherty's initial briefing had been refreshingly upbeat, chairman Peter Mead's first statement directly to Millwall's fans was understandably sombre, but nevertheless, typically optimistic:

"It was a deeply upsetting day on Monday when people had to lose their jobs to help break the circle of losses which have surrounded the club for a number of years now and which have only been offset by player sales. Two particular regrets of mine have been the departure of Graham Hortop and Jimmy Nicholl. Graham has been incredibly diligent and loyal to me and to my predecessors and I feel his loss deeply. As far as Jimmy is concerned, it is easy to say now that hiring Jimmy was a mistake. But I still believe that wasn't the case and that circumstances conspired against him, not least the crippling injury list we have had for much of the season. I think Jimmy Nicholl is a very decent man and will go on to be successful elsewhere. Having said that, I know many supporters have been hankering after what they would describe as a return to the Millwall spirit, the pride and the passion. It seemed to all of us that once you acknowledge that things have got to change, a new team built around people we know from the old days who believe in the club should be the way forward. To suggest that there was some sort of conspiracy is not true at all. The first time I spoke to John Docherty was last Friday when I asked him to come up and see me on Sunday to talk about a possibility which had emerged. We spoke at some length and then talked to David Buchler, and it was only then that John readily agreed to accept the challenge. John certainly is no stranger to working in the face of adversity. His marvellous achievement in getting Millwall promoted to the old First Division in 1988 may cause people to forget that when he first came here his major accomplishment was stabilising the situation then and bringing out the best from the resources he had. During that time he was also planning for the future and that historic season, and please God that will happen again. In the longer term I have always admired the Liverpool way of doing

things where they seem to produce from within dyed in the wool Liverpool people, and I would personally view it as a wonderful thing if John were able to nurture say Keith Stevens through to a much higher profile management role over the next few years. But that is one of the issues we'll get round to facing when we've sorted out the short term, beginning hopefully with a return to winning ways this afternoon."

Mead's statement revealed two very key points: the first was, as fans had known deep down since day one, player sales in recent seasons were made mainly to balance the books and not to reinvigorate the squad. The very nature of buying and selling players for "undisclosed" fees is that fans never get to find out just how little their prized assets have been given away for - or the truth behind how much has been reinvested in the team or actually disappeared down a black hole of debt. Of course, with the club being listed on the stock exchange, its financial washing was aired annually for all to gawp at.

The departure of Hortop, a diligent and loyal club servant who had served Millwall through good times and bad, was also a sad indication of just how parlous The Lions' financial plight had become. A few fans may have raised an incredulous eyebrow at Mead's closing statement about doing things 'the Liverpool way', although in fairness to him, the re-appointment of John Docherty who in turn gave lifelong club stalwart Keith 'Rhino' Stevens a coaching role, was in line with how the Anfield club had nurtured their unprecedented success through the late seventies and all of the eighties and, right now, was exactly the direction to ease Millwall into. The Stevens move would prove to be a key element in the club's long, long road to eventual recovery but that was still some way off, with the immediate future frighteningly uncertain.

True to his reputation, Docherty was quickly able to

mould his limited resources into a stubborn, hard-to-beat unit and his first three matches produced a 2-0 home win over Rotherham in his first match back at the club, a 1-1 draw away to Shrewsbury and 1-0 at home against Notts County. All of the goals in those three matches came in the final ten minutes, a welcome break from what Lions fans had been accustomed to in recent weeks when matches were lost by half time. Finally, there was an air of cautious optimism about the place. Docherty's impact had been positive and immediate, Millwall were back in the promotion places and, following the age-old formula of winning home games and drawing away, could The Doc pull off the unthinkable and win promotion for Millwall again?

South Bermondsey homesick blues

16

reality bites

March 1997...
Third tier Chesterfield reach the FA Cup semi-
final;
Joe Royle resigns as Everton manager;
160 vehicles are involved in a motorway pile up on
the M42 motorway. Three people are killed and 60
injured;
PM John Major announces that the general election
will be held on 1 May;
Beatle Paul McCartney receives his knighthood
from the Queen;
The Spice Girls launch Britain's new television
channel, Channel 5...

The Docherty effect was showing no signs of wearing off as Millwall started March with wins against struggling Wycombe Wanderers and second placed Luton. Despite suggesting that, due to the club's long injury list, the team would 'pick itself' and there would be little change to personnel, The Doc performed major surgery on Millwall's flimsy defence, bolstering it with the experience of Greg Berry, Tony Witter and a player who had been part of the super-sturdy back four in Docherty's triumphant Second Division champions back in 1988 and their tumultuous top flight debut: Alan McLeary.

Wycombe were beaten 2-1 at The Den thanks to goals

from Hartley and Dolby but the stand-out performance of the season had to be at Kenilworth Road where the same two players scored again in the final ten minutes to leave The Lions breathing down the necks of second-placed Luton and inflict the in-form Hatters' first defeat in twelve matches. The form team in Division Two was now clear - it was John Docherty's Lions with four wins and a draw from his five matches since taking over. While the spectre of extinction still lurked ominously at the season's end, it would be easier to banish with the club having won promotion - however unlikely that still felt. When mid-table Bournemouth arrived at The Den, the momentum Millwall had gathered under Docherty looked to be timed perfectly for an assault on the top two automatic promotion places as the season entered the home straight:

Nationwide League Division Two - March 14th 1997						
	P	W	D	L	F	A	PTS
1. Brentford	34	16	13	5	50	31	61
2. Luton	34	16	9	9	57	39	57
3. MILLWALL	**35**	**16**	**9**	**10**	**46**	**43**	**57**

Docherty's strength in his first spell as Millwall manager had been his faith in youth and the Luton victory had seen a first team debut for another young player when striker Richard Sadlier came on as a second half sub and he made his full debut at The Den as Millwall looked to put further pressure on the top two.

With Brentford losing their unbeaten home record in a surprise 3-0 reverse to Burnley and Luton being held 0-0 by Crewe the opportunity was there to grab second place - and with an out-of-sorts Brentford facing Luton next, top spot was up for grabs.

The nature of Bournemouth's 1-0 win, with the deciding goal arriving with just over ten minutes left was a jarringly familiar scenario for the bumper crowd that had turned up at

The Den hoping to see the latest instalment of the Docherty fairy tale. A resolute 0-0 draw with Crewe followed but another 1-0 home defeat - this time to a Watford side who, like a number of other clubs were making their own late dash for the top spots, put Millwall's promotion aspirations well and truly into perspective. Goals had once more deserted them and yet, inkeeping with a season that was as unpredictable as it had been frustrating, a Good Friday trip across the border to north Wales saw a The Lions share six goals with Wrexham. Going into the break 3-1 down, the travelling Millwall supporters must have been fearing a repeat of the Stockport debacle but were treated to a heartening second half comeback with goals from Newman and a Rogan penalty sealing a remarkable recovery and end the month with them still clinging precariously to a play-off spot in sixth place.

Unfortunately, that was to be virtually the last Millwall fans had to cheer and that encouraging league position was soon to fade badly.

April 1997...
Bolton win promotion to the Premier League;
Leicester win the Coca Cola League Cup final,
beating Middlesbrough 1-0 after extra time
courtesy of a Steve Claridge goal;
The last MORI poll before the election tips Labour
for a landslide victory as they gain 48% of the
vote and a 20-point lead over the Conservatives...

From day one, Millwall knew they had the best possible chance to win promotion at the first attempt and regain their First Division place that had been so cruelly snatched from them. In what appeared to be one of the most open divisions of football in decades, all The Lions needed was to find some consistency at any stage of the season to build a promotion-winning lead at the top of the table. It was a table that had been led from the start by a totally unremarkable Brentford side who were built on physical strength and direct play and, once they lost their unbeaten home record, fell away as many expected. Their only challenge had come from Luton who recovered from a patchy start and looked a good bet to nick the title after being the team to break that Brentford home record. The most consistent of the play-off contenders it seemed was Watford.

As it transpired, it was indeed to prove the most open promotion race in recent years and it was three teams who had barely troubled the top places until the crucial run-in that would eventually win promotion.

Bury, who had been on the fringe of the play-off picture without ever managing to establish themselves in it clicked at just the right time, winning nine of their last 13 matches to take the championship. Similarly, Stockport, who were floundering in the lower reaches of the league when they hit Millwall for four and then five goals in their two league meetings, surged from seventh place in late March to claim the runners-up spot behind their neighbours. Completing the promotion picture's north-westerly theme was a Crewe side who, despite only managing to win once in their last five matches and having been beaten 6-0 away to Luton when in mid-table a few months before, eased into the play-offs' final berth with a paltry 73 points - yet four clear of nearest rivals Blackpool. The fact that Crewe's play-off success came at the expense of long time top two dwellers Luton and then Brentford told you all you needed to know about how open the division had been.

For Millwall, the season petered out dreadfully with just two points and a solitary goal from their last seven matches. Damien Webber's last minute equaliser to secure a 1-1 draw at home to relegation-haunted York in the first match of April was the last goal Lions fans were able to celebrate. Nine unbearable hours of football followed where 1-0 defeats to Burnley, Bristol Rovers and Chesterfield, a 2-0 home loss to Gillingham and a goalless draw at Plymouth rounded off an utterly miserable month and send them spiralling down to 14th place in the table.

May 1997...
Brighton survive relegation out of the Football League on the final day as Hereford go down; Chelsea beat Middlesbrough 2-0 to win the FA Cup; The UK win The Eurovision Song Contest with Katrina and the Waves singing Love Shine A Light; The Labour Party under Tony Blair defeat the incumbent Conservative government under Prime Minister John Major in a landslide result, winning 418 seats...

There are few more disheartening experiences for a football fan than being at another team's promotion party. It had been a season where, as with the previous one, Millwall had looked a good bet for a promotion place only to slide unerringly down the table. Whilst they had avoided the disaster of relegation that slide had led to twelve months earlier but had suffered the arguably far more debilitating and potentially terminal fate of entering administration, the handful of hardy souls that made the trip to Bury's Gigg Lane to see their team easily beaten 2-0 in the Shakers' championship parade must have felt a sickening feeling in the pit of their stomachs similar to that after the corresponding match at Ipswich the season before when news sunk in that their beloved Millwall had been relegated.

Millwall's final placing of 14th with 61 points was just 14 above relegated Peterborough - a side who had taken four points off The Lions and knocked them out of the League Cup. Yet Crewe, who had taken the final play-off place and gone on to win promotion at Wembley had finished a mere 12 points ahead of Docherty's side. After that impressive 2-0 away to Luton which should have proved the catalyst for Millwall's promotion charge, no further matches were won in the final eleven matches where just four points were gained from a possible 33. Had The Lions been able to adhere to that age-old promotion formula of winning at home and drawing away in those last eleven matches, the 21 points won would have seen them tied on points with runners-up Stockport - although with an inferior goal difference, missing out on automatic promotion by such a fine margin twelve months after being relegated in similar circumstances might have been a bit much for Millwall fans to bear!

A far better perspective to take is that, were it not for administration and ultimately the sacking of Jimmy Nicholl, without that 13 point run coming at the start of John Docherty's return to the hot seat, those same long-suffering fans may well have been spending the summer contemplating watching their team compete in the bottom tier of English football.

As it stood, whether there would be a team to watch at all was still very much in the balance. Millwall had fulfilled its obligation to the football authorities to complete the 1996-97 season, but now those same authorities would be pressing them to confirm they would be in a fit state to begin the next. As it stood, the answer appeared to be "no".

As Lions fans made the long journey back to London with the spring sunshine slowly setting on a Bury promotion party that would run long into the night, they wondered if they had watched The Lions for the final time. Salvation was relatively simple, Millwall needed a new owner. The reality was, finding someone to buy a football club was one thing, finding someone to buy Millwall Football Club with all its associated baggage was an entirely different proposition.

Millwall needed a miracle.

The fortunate reality for Millwall fans was that, during the weeks and months that immediately followed the shock plunging of the club into administration, a very keen buyer was eagerly waiting in the wings and frantic efforts had been going on behind the scenes - and closely monitored by The South London Press - to save the club and stabilise it under new ownership.

That did not detract from the fact that the club did indeed come very close to going out of business. It was a fact that was easier to conceal from concerned fans - and more importantly its many detractors who would happily have seen it cease to exist. Without the added spotlight of the Internet, its chat forums, ubiquitous news updates and social media to feed the vultures, Millwall were able to be given the vital kiss of life with far fewer morbid onlookers.

That kiss of life was delivered, in the main, by one man: Theo Paphitis. A name not heard before in footballing circles - although some years earlier he had invested in his local club Walton and Hersham. Once the formalities of the old season were disposed of and the various require-ments of the Football League had been met, Paphitis quickly showed that his tenure as Lions owner would be very different to any other that Millwall fans had known. With ink on contracts and agreements still damp, Paphitis made his first move as Millwall chairman: Manager John Docherty had left and in his place was a name that shocked The Lions' long-suffering supporters to their core.

It was a name that was legendary in London football - at least for one particular part of London, but certainly not the Millwall part...

Nationwide League Division Two Final Table 1996-97

	Team	Pld	W	D	L	GF	GA	GD	Pts
1	**Bury**	46	24	12	10	62	38	+24	84
2	**Stockport County**	46	23	13	10	59	41	+18	82
3	Luton Town	46	21	15	10	71	45	+26	78
4	Brentford	46	20	14	12	56	43	+13	74
5	Bristol City	46	21	10	15	69	51	+18	73
6	**Crewe Alexandra**	46	22	7	17	56	47	+9	73
7	Blackpool	46	18	15	13	60	47	+13	69
8	Wrexham	46	17	18	11	55	50	+5	69
9	Burnley	46	19	11	16	71	55	+16	68
10	Chesterfield	46	18	14	14	42	39	+3	68
11	Gillingham	46	19	10	17	60	59	+1	67
12	Walsall	46	19	10	17	54	53	+1	67
13	Watford	46	16	19	11	45	38	+7	67
14	**Millwall**	**46**	**16**	**13**	**17**	**50**	**55**	**−5**	**61**
15	Preston North End	·46	18	7	21	49	55	−6	61
16	Bournemouth	46	15	15	16	43	45	−2	60
17	Bristol Rovers	46	15	11	20	47	50	−3	56
18	Wycombe Wanderers	46	15	10	21	51	57	−6	55
19	Plymouth Argyle	46	12	18	16	47	58	−11	54
20	York City	46	13	13	20	47	68	−21	52
21	**Peterborough United**	46	11	14	21	55	73	−18	47
22	**Shrewsbury Town**	46	11	13	22	49	74	−25	46
23	**Rotherham United**	46	7	14	25	39	70	−31	35
24	**Notts County**	46	7	14	25	33	59	−26	35

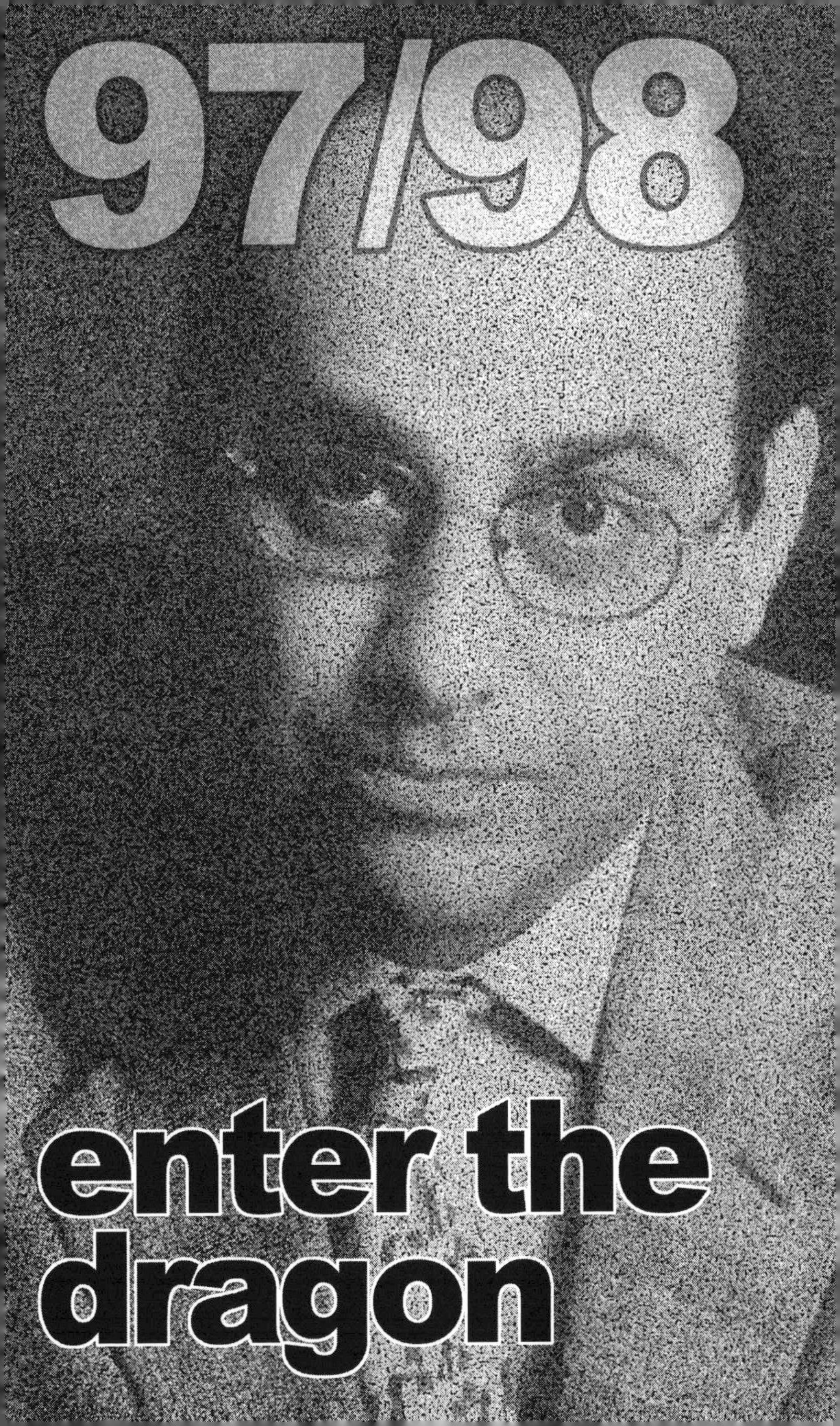
97/98
enter the dragon

SOUTH BERMONDSEY HOMESICK BLUES

17

a change in the weather

June 1997...
The Football league announce that replays in the
League Cup will be scrapped from next season;
Manchester United sign Teddy Sheringham from
Tottenham for £3.5m; QPR sign striker Mike Sheron
from Stoke for £2.5m...
Harry Potter and The Philosopher's Stone, written
by J.K. Rowling is published; Legendary Manchester
venue The Hacienda closes its doors for the final
time...
July 1997...
Homeless Brighton announce plans to ground-
share with Gillingham and then Millwall after
surviving an attempt to expel them from the league
for a late bond payment of £500,000...
Chancellor Gordon Brown launches the first
Labour budget for nearly 20 years...

Just five days after that season-ending defeat at Bury,
Millwall had seen a new owner arrive and make his first big
move. Theo Paphitis proved that he would be a proactive
chairman and wasn't afraid to make footballing decisions
as well as financial and commercial ones. He also proved
that, despite the ferocious reputation of Millwall's support,
he wasn't afraid to make controversial ones, and they didn't
come more controversial than the managerial appointment

of one of the all time supporter favourites of The Lions' bitterest rivals: Billy Bonds.

Understandably Millwall supporters' reaction was far from subdued with most being horrified at the prospect of cheering on a team picked by a man almost as symbolic with their arch rivals West Ham as 1966 World Cup heroes Moore and Hurst.

Opinion ranged from the few who accepted how close the club had come to going out of business and were prepared to accept anything to see Millwall still playing football come August - to those at the other end of the outrage scale who vowed never to set foot inside The Den again, citing Paphitis' arrival as some kind of inside job by their foes from across the river to bury them for good.

Somewhere in the middle, once the initial shock had subsided, there was a group of fans that did accept that Bonds' managerial CV was, whilst sparse, virtually perfect. He had masterminded the promotion of his beloved West Ham to the top flight some six years earlier - largely at the expense of Millwall's own promotion ambitions at the time. It was a hell of a stretch, but if he could repeat the process at The Den and get Millwall back into football's second tier there might be some room for forgiveness and acceptance but, make no mistake, this was a managerial appointment up there with Clough to Leeds.

With the new season fast approaching, Millwall fans had little time to dwell on the Bonds appointment. Paphitis' whirlwind was, it seemed, unceasing. A new kit, complete with new shirt sponsor quickly followed and, in a similar vein to his choice of manager, Paphitis seemed to enjoy pulling a surprise that brought with it, a degree of positive publicity.

OK so maybe the new shirts which matched the traditional Millwall blue with a silvery grey instead of white wasn't going to have the new Labour government being asked for explanations at Prime Minister's Question Time, but it was certainly another eyebrow-raiser.

More so was the choice of sponsor. Those new shirts were emblazoned with the bizarre logo of L!VE TV (exclamation mark well and truly intended) bordered top and bottom by the intriguing strapline of "The Weather in Norwegian".

1997 saw the start of the TV revolution. For the last few years, a privileged few had access to what was then known as cable television. It was a medium - with access to 100s of channels - that had been commonplace in the USA for years (of course) but attempts to replicate it this side of the Atlantic had stalled somewhat since BSB and Sky made the initial moves in the late 80s. Backed by Murdoch's megabucks, BSB and Sky merged and now the service was gaining momentum. Where previously you had to be chosen to have your front path dug up and cables sunk into it to have the handful of decidedly iffy new channels piped in, now the service was more slick with the sort of dedicated sports and film output that the US enjoyed delivered through a satellite bolted to your chimney stack.

As take-up steadily increased and the nation's telly addicts embraced increasingly easy access to more than just the usual four, more channels started to appear virtually overnight.

In a move almost certainly a reaction to Murdoch's emergence as the new service's prime mover, rival The Mirror Group set up L!VE TV in 1995 headed by Kelvin MacKenzie with Janet Street-Porter as managing director. Street-Porter left within months after disagreements with MacKenzie over content, leaving him to oversee altogether more, shall we say, selective programming that, it would turn out, be right up Millwall's alley in terms of dividing public opinion.

Output included Topless Darts where semi-naked models threw arrows on the beach; Britain's Bounciest Weather with Rusty Goffe (who appeared as an Oompa Loompa in the 1971 film Willy Wonka & the Chocolate Factory) who, due to his small stature, bounced on a trampoline while doing the forecast (bouncing higher the further up north he was talking about) Tiffany's Big City Tips, in which model Tiffany Banister gave the financial news while stripping to her underwear; Painted Ladies, which involved topless girls "painting" on large sheets of paper with various body parts; The News Bunny, a person in a rabbit suit who stood behind a newsreader making gestures and expressions for each item, and the weather read in Norwegian by model Anne-Marie Foss. You can probably see the link here. Imagine Carry On meets Panto season.

The new kit and sponsor were unveiled to what was by now an incredulous Millwall support who were reeling at the pace at which these sweeping changes were coming at them. After so many seasons of stagnation, decay, empty promises and a distinct grey gloom dripping from every orifice at The Den, a pitch photocall saw new boss Bonds posing somewhat awkwardly in his smart Chinos with a rampant Lion incongruously roaring from the left breast of his club polo. Flanked by models Foss and Kirsten Imrie (the former Page Three favourite was L!VE TV's sports anchor - of course) who were modelling the new home and away strip, this was both the stuff of Millwall fan fantasy and nightmare. Some must have felt they had mistakenly ingested a long lost stash of pills from the 1988 heyday and were having a dodgy trip, especially when "The News Bunny" was then joined by Zampa The Lion alongside Chairman Theo.

Word was of course now doing the rounds and whilst in some rival fan quarters the club were being seen as something as a laughing stock in both their choice of manager and shirt sponsor, the shrewd Paphitis will have surely savoured the fact that, for once, Millwall's publicity wasn't all bad.

By the time the season's opener at home to Brentford had arrived the fans had to swallow a few more bitter pills. A 4-0 home friendly pasting by Palace followed by the arrival of ex-West Ham veterans Kenny Brown and Paul Allen to the playing staff, coupled with the departure of club legends Bob Pearson and Kevin O'Callaghan meant that the 8,000 or so Lions fans that were there to witness the start of this new era in the history of the club did so with more reservations than expectation.

SOUTH BERMONDSEY HONESTY BLUES

18

BONdiNg...

August 1997...
Teddy Sheringham misses a penalty for Manchester
United on his return to Tottenham but his side run
out 2-0 winners; 1,073 fans watch Brighton draw 1-1
with Orient in their first game sharing Gillingham's Priestfield Stadium, while plans to share
The Den with Millwall appear doomed with Police
opposition...
Princess Diana dies after the car she was
travelling in as a passenger crashes in a Paris
tunnel while allegedly trying to evade pursuing
photographers...

If there was one aspect of Theo Paphitis' arrival that
fans did welcome, it was the making available of
funds for essential squad building. As both Paphitis
and Bonds were to soon discover however, having money
to spend doesn't automatically mean you can sign players.

Bonds spoke of his frustration at trying to do deals for
new blood on the season's eve in his first ever Millwall
programme notes as his first Lions line-up relied heavily
on youth for goals. Youngsters Richard Sadlier and Danny
Hockton were teamed up with the more experienced Kim
Grant who had arrived on loan from Luton. Grant had been
a thorn in Millwall's side during his days with Charlton and

had a scoring pedigree that was evident when, just after the hour mark, he scored to give The Lions a 3-0 lead over Brentford - and Bonds the perfect start. Millwall had held a narrow advantage at the break after taking a fortunate 22nd-minute thanks to a Jamie Bates own goal. To add to the unfamiliarity, fans were deprived of their usual routine of seeing The Lions attack The Cold Blow Lane end as the sides resumed for the second period but were quickly celebrating a second goal when the impressive Sadlier began and finished a move that saw him latch onto a booming Tim Carter clearance, play the ball out to Savage on the right and finish the return ball smartly the put The Lions in control. It was one of Millwall's most commanding opening day performances in years and went a little way to the fans accepting their new manager - although the sight of 'Bonzo' in the Lions' dugout would still take some getting used to...

Grant was on target again in the midweek League Cup first round first leg trip to Northampton but two strikes in five second half minutes saw Bonds taste defeat for the first time ahead of the league trip to Preston.

Richard Sadlier, the youngster scouted from Irish football, was by his own admission, ready to pack his bags and return to Ireland just months before. A mixture of home-sickness and the assumption that he'd be made redundant as part of the club's scathing administration-enforced cuts should have seen him back across the Irish Channel. Various factors kept him at the club, where managers John Docherty and Billy Bonds both recognised the value of nurturing young talent and, after opening his league account in that first match at The Den, he made a stunning, immediate impact at Deepdale with a spectacular strike from 30 yards out to give his side a sixth-minute lead.

Unfortunately, Millwall's soft defensive underbelly was once again exposed as goals either side of half time saw them slip to a 2-1 defeat at a venue they had rarely enjoyed success. The rollercoaster continued back at home when the impressive Grant first gave Millwall the lead against York and then clawed it back to 2-2 after The Lions' leaky defence was breached all too easily again, only for ex-Millwall winger Paul Stephenson to inflict a third straight defeat with a later winner.

As expected, Lions fans would be much quicker to turn on a manager who had slept with the enemy and their patience appeared to snap four days later. Despite another encouraging attacking display from the third of their new-look strikeforce, Danny Hockton's second half salvo was cancelled out by a last-minute Gayle goal for North-ampton in the League Cup first round second leg, taking the tie into extra time.

The match was eventually won somewhat comically 2-0 on a penalty shootout, but a month that had started with so much promise was beginning to take on a familiar look.

September 1997...
Bolton's Reebok Stadium is the fourth new football ground to open in recent months following Sunder-land's Stadium of Light, Derby's Pride Park and Stoke's Britannia Stadium; England just need a draw in Rome against Italy in the final qualifier in October to make it to the World Cup in France next year;
Elton John performs 'Candle in the Wind' at the Funeral of Diana, Princess of Wales;
Seven die and 139 are injured in the Southall rail crash when a Passenger train passes a danger signal and collides with a freight train.

Millwall travelled to Luton in a familiar position in the Division Two table - just above the relegation zone, yet things were about to take a very encouraging turn.

Sandwiched by an international break and a 5-1 home battering by Wimbledon in the League Cup second round,

Millwall managed to chalk up three consecutive wins with a 2-0 victory at Luton, a 3-1 success at home to Southend and rare three points away to Grimsby. The goals were shared amongst the increasingly impressive Hockton and Sadlier, although Grant's goals had appeared to dry up at around the same time the ink did on his contract after making his Luton loan move permanent off the back of that early flurry of goals.

Making a goalscoring debut against the team where his career began in that 1-0 win at Grimsby was another striker. Veteran frontman Paul Wilkinson had joined from Barnsley with an impressive career of goals at the top level for Everton, Nottingham Forest and Watford and his goals-coring Lions bow saw his new side hit the play-off places ahead of a trip to seventh-placed Northampton where the mini run came to and end in a disappointingly tame 2-0 defeat. Wimbledon completed a 9-2 League Cup second round aggregate rout where few tears were shed at exiting the competition by 3,500 Den diehards to end another month on another bum note.

19

IN THE BLACK...

October 1997...
Captained by a bloodied Paul Ince, reminiscent of
Terry Butcher's performance in another World Cup
qualifier back in 1989, England reach France 98
with a 0-0 draw against Italy in Rome.

Keen to continue adding to his squad, Billy Bonds
brought in Michael Black - a young winger on
loan from Arsenal. Millwall fans had always
enjoyed exciting, tricky players and Black was an instant
hit, instrumental in another goal for Wilkinson - enabling
the veteran to join that exclusive club of scoring on both
his Millwall home and away debuts. The 2-1 victory
was sealed by a welcome return to goalscoring form by
Kim Grant and enabled Millwall to leapfrog opponents
Blackpool and back into the top six. Meanwhile, never
bothering to allowing the facts to get in the way of a good
story, the national press were suggesting that Paphitis'
takeover wasn't all it seemed and that the club were still
in financial difficulty. In the programme for that Blackpool
victory, Paphitis was quick to squash the story in his
unique, no-nonsense style:

*"Due to the Administration, we have had to extend our
accounting period from the 31st May 1997 to the 30th*

November 1997 in order to include all the crap left over during Administration..."

Crap indeed...

Millwall fans may not have understood Theo's explanation of the ins and outs of the City, CVAs and other such matters, but they will have appreciated the cut of his gib in that first paragraph alone. So, back in the black, and fresh from returning to winning ways against Blackpool, it was fitting that new man Michael Black would celebrate his explosive start to life with The Lions with the winning goal as Millwall came from behind to beat Oldham 2-1 at The Den and send Bonds' boys up to third in the table ahead of a crucial clash at table-topping Watford and a trip to fourth-placed Bournemouth.

A single goal from Paul Shaw at Vicarage Road sealed one of Millwall's most impressive away victories in years and equally professional was the resolute defensive display in a 0-0 draw by the coast that saw them cement a top four spot. With home matches against mid-table Wigan and seventh-placed Bristol City, surely it was only a matter of time before Watford's table-topping lead was whittled away further and The Lions could get a firm foothold on those precious automatic promotion places.

Nationwide League Division Two - October 29th 1997						
	P	W	D	L	F	A	PTS
1. Watford	14	10	2	2	23	10	32
2. Northampton	14	7	5	2	16	9	26
3. Gillingham	14	7	3	4	21	15	24
4. MILLWALL	**12**	**7**	**2**	**3**	**18**	**11**	**23**
5. Oldham	14	5	6	3	23	20	21
5. York	14	6	3	5	20	19	21

Lions fans are only too aware of course of the dangers of looking too far ahead or anticipating success. Bobby Bowry scored a last kick goal in the Wigan clash - but only after Graeme Jones had given The Latics an 86th-minute lead and worse was to follow four days later when the second of Millwall's ghosts of its top flight days would return to haunt it.

Striker Steve Torpey had broken into the first team after the departure of Tony Cascarino back in 1990 having progressed through The Lions' youth ranks but had failed to claim a regular place and became part of John Docherty's player exodus, joining the Scot at Bradford. Now established in Bristol City's frontline, he joined Paul Stephenson as one of two players to appear for Millwall in the top tier - and score against them in the third.

Fans were quick once more to jump on the players' and managers' back as the teams left the pitch at the end of that 2-0 defeat to Bristol City, something which, for the first time, Bonds displayed his disappointment at in his programme notes for the next home game. Were the cracks beginning to show already?

November 1997...
The last unbeaten record in the league goes with Arsenal's 3-0 defeat to Derby; Ron Atkinson returns to manage Sheffield Wednesday after the sacking of David Pleat.
The Prodigy release their controversial single "Smack My Bitch Up", which is censored by Radio 1 and the X-rated video is banned from daytime television, except for a brief, late night rotation on MTV before being removed from broadcast 2 weeks later; Brazil's Supreme Court refuses to extradite the Great Train Robber Ronnie Biggs to Britain; Six Britons are among the 58 people killed by terrorists in the Valley of the Kings, Egypt; The Queen and The Duke of Edinburgh celebrate their 50th wedding anniversary.

Bonds had every right to test the Millwall fans' reaction to his first negative thoughts on their relationship. By the time he'd penned his programme notes for the first home match of November against Kevin Keegan's nouveau riche Fulham, his side had once again displayed their resilience to bounce back and turn on the style against their promotion rivals away from The Den. Back down in fifth place, they travelled to fourth-placed Gillingham who were one of the form sides of the division and unbeaten at home. After weathering an early storm, Michael Black gave Millwall a first half lead, only for them to be pegged back when Leo Fortune-West equalised with just over twenty minutes left and with The Gills in the ascendency despite being reduced to ten men following the dismissal of Statham after a second yellow, there only seemed to be one winner.

Paul Shaw was causing the stretched Kent side's defence all sorts of problems as the game entered its last ten minutes and the tide finally turned when the former Arsenal striker regained The Lions' lead in the 83rd minute with a typically cool finish and Wilkinson added some last-minute gloss with his and Millwall's third goal.

Fulham arrived at The Den freshly buoyed by the millions invested by Harrods owner Mohammed Al Fayed and with a coaching dream team of Keegan and Ray Wilkins. Millwall's best crowd of the season of over 10,000 saw Paul Peschisolido give Keegan's men what looked to be the match-winning lead just after half time, but it was that man Shaw again who popped up to save a point with three minutes left.

Millwall's home form continued to give cause for concern however as they slipped further behind the top two with another home draw, this time against struggling Carlisle who salvaged a point late on with a last gasp Matt Jansen goal to leave The Lions without a home success in four as Bonds took his side into their FA Cup campaign.

The next few weeks would see Millwall loathe the very mention of the word 'Bristol', with a cup clash away to

City, a league trip to Rovers and Boxing Day trip back at City returning absolutely nothing. Whilst disposing of the distraction of the League Cup was acceptable, the FA Cup was a very different matter. Both in terms of the excitement of the possibility of a big name draw in the third round and the financial benefits that would bring, to surrender that opportunity so meekly 1-0 was tough to take.

Millwall's joy on the road continued however with a return to league action and winning ways thanks to goals from Bowry and Savage to give them a 2-1 win at Burnley and send them back up to third place, but that homesickness returned with a desperately disappointing 1-1 draw with sixth-placed Chesterfield. In an under-standably tight encounter between two play-off contenders looking to break into the automatic promotion places, Millwall seemed to have finally made the breakthrough after pounding on The Spireites' door for an hour as Shaw grabbed his third goal in the five league starts, but just eight minutes later The Lions nodded off once more to allow Perkins to snatch a leveller.

Another frustrating month ended with another fruitless trip to Bristol where Shaw was again on target. This time however, his 60th-minute equaliser was wiped out by Barry Hayles' winner for Rovers ten minutes from time. Remarkably, Millwall remained in third place, however their erratic form and failure to win at home in almost two months meant that, even at this relatively early stage with more than half of the season still to play, they were a full ten points adrift of second placed Bristol City and sixteen behind Graham Taylor's table-topping Watford. Two wins in nine league games since that victory at Vicarage Road that had seen them reduce The Hornets' lead to three points wasn't promotion form. It was mid-table, and that's precisely where Billy Bonds' Lions were heading.

SOUth BeUmoUdsey homesick BlUes

20

GraY days

December 1997...
Charlton player Jamie Stuart fails a drug test and
is suspended by the club pending an FA inquiry;
Jurgen Klinsmann returns to Tottenham as does
David Pleat as director of football.
Andrew Evans, who was convicted of the 1972
murder of 14-year-old Judith Roberts in Tamworth,
Staffordshire, has his conviction overturned by
the Court of Appeal...

December started with news that one of Millwall's legion
of West Ham old boys had left the club. Bonds' assistant and
former Hammers team-mate Pat Holland made the move to
Spurs as their Under-19s coach. Often the departure of a
manager's right hand man results in a dip in results and the
position is a much-underrated one.

It's unlikely that Millwall supporters who trudged away
from The Den after another numbing defeat - this time
to the only goal of the game against struggling Walsall
- would have made the connection between Holland's
departure and The Lions' apparent nosedive in form. It
was nothing new - especially in a decade that had so far
produced, almost every season, a promising opening,
followed by an inexplicable loss of form to dash promotion
hopes - or even result in a relegation scrap.

Shaw and Grant found the target in a 2-0 Auto Windscreens Shield tie victory away to Cardiff meaning that Bonds had tasted defeat just twice on his travels in seven league and cup matches - both at Bristol. Not that Millwall fans were bothered about what they saw as a pointless lower league cup competition, despite it offering a Wembley final, but they soon would.

If The Lions were flattering to deceive by clinging on to third place, that deception was soon blasted wide open when they travelled to a Plymouth side down in 20th position and with just four wins to their name all season and were blown away 3-0. With the busy Christmas period fast approaching, Millwall had picked the worst possible time to lose form.

Shaw was on target yet again as victory at home was finally tasted for the first time in almost three months with a 1-0 win over Wycombe but if any supporters were kidding themselves that the blip had been ridden out, they were given a rude awakening over the festive break when first Bristol City inflicted a 4-1 thrashing at Ashton Gate on Boxing Day and Luton stole all the points with two goals in the last two minutes at The Den to put those promotion aspirations well and truly in perspective. In the blink of an eye Millwall had gone from being play-off challengers to mid-table also-rans and even though the door to that end of season lottery remains ajar to almost all sides until late in the season, only the most optimistic of Lions follower would really expect them to mount any sort of challenge given their seemingly complete loss of form - and fortune.

Young strike duo Sadlier and Hockton had succumbed to long term injury and loss of form and their replacements Grant and Wilkinson could not buy a goal, leaving scoring duties squarely at the feet of Paul Shaw and, were it not for his crucial goals, would have seen Millwall plunged into another relegation fight. Just to rub salt in their wounds, if

Millwall fans had started to console themselves with the possibility of a trip to Wembley in the Auto Windscreens Shield instead of the play-offs, they were delivered the news they didn't want to hear: Millwall's first match of 1998 would be an AWS tie - away to Bristol City.

January 1998...
Paul Gascoigne apologises for his 'flute-playing' mime in Rangers' clash with Celtic and donates his £20,000 club fine to charity; The Euro 2000 quali-fying draw sees England face Poland for the fifth time running in a major qualifying competition. Non-league Stevenage Borough hold Premier League Newcastle to a 1-1 draw in the FA Cup fourth round.

With the honeymoon period - if ever there was one - well and truly over, Billy Bonds finally addressed the elephant in the room in his programme notes for Millwall's home league match against Wrexham:

"I don't think I'm ever going to be the most popular manager who has ever been at Millwall because of my West Ham background, but I do genuinely want to do well for this club and especially for the supporters who have been marvellous to me since I've been here..."

As bizarre as that may have sounded, it was probably true. The individual fans that Bonds may have encountered in the club car park before and after matches would almost certainly have been supportive, given the steady start made to the season by a makeshift squad. In small numbers, away from the pressure-cooker environment of the match itself, football fans are generally a forgiving bunch. But in large numbers, as they stare another home defeat in the face or hear the referee's whistle end another numbing ninety minutes, patience snaps and opinions are voiced as one.

With the 1-0 AWS defeat at Bristol taking The Lions' miserable run of form to six defeats in seven and Millwall down in twelfth position, their Welsh opponents arrived just one place below them and took full advantage of

Millwall's malaise, grabbing a 1-0 win to leave Bonds' men closer to the relegation places than the promotion ones. When they went in at half time a goal behind at York City a week later they were, quite inconceivably, heading for the bottom four and Lions fans sipping their half time Bovril on that cold January terrace in Yorkshire must have been having nightmarish flashbacks of 1996 and contemplating Millwall's first visit to the Football League basement since 1964.

Fortunately, Billy Bonds had pulled off a masterstroke in the transfer market the week before in bringing in stalwart midfielder Andy Gray. The ex-Palace and Villa man had a fearsome reputation as a ruthless enforcer, coupled with deft ball skills and a footballing brain way beyond third tier level. In a midfield display reminiscent of Millwall legend Terry Hurlock, Gray quickly settled into his Lions debut and was running the show as the second half wore on. Grant equalised within three minutes of the restart and Shaw edged his side ahead just past the hour mark. Although Bull seemed to have nicked a point for The Minstermen in the last minute, Gray inspired his new teammates to battle back and Shaw popped up with the injury time winner.

The addition of Andy Gray was exactly what Millwall had been missing all season. A mainstay to protect a narrow lead, regain victory from the jaws of defeat and settle nerves when up against it. He had been part of the dream trio at Crystal Palace when, alongside Ian Wright and Mark Bright, he had led The Eagles to their best ever top flight finish.

On the scoresheet again for York that day was Paul Stephenson. The Geordie wonderkid who, along with Paul Gascoigne and Ian Bogie, had come through the Newcastle youth ranks and promised to be one of the footballing stars of the future. Out of Wright, Bright, Gray, Gascoigne, Stephenson and Bogie, four had, over the last decade, pulled on a Millwall shirt. That they did in either the Autumn of their careers (as was the case with Bright and Gray) or in the raw Spring of ultimately unfulfilled promise in the case of Stephenson and Bogie, said a lot for Millwall's fortunes in that ten years. So much promise, with nothing to show for it.

A point next in a goalless draw at struggling Southend was perhaps a prime example of how a player like Gray made the difference between a point gained and going home empty-handed. Sadly, the upside of Gray's years of experience was tempered by the downside of his advancing years meaning absence through injury was never far away.

February 1998...
Northern Ireland name Lawrie McMenemy as their new manager; Steve Bull scores his 300th goal for Wolves; Barnsley knock favourites Manchester United out of the FA Cup.
Danbert Nobacon of Chumbawamba pours a bucket of ice over UK Deputy Prime Minister John Prescott at the 1998 Brit Awards; Great Britain and Northern Ireland compete at the Winter Olympics in Nagano, Japan, and win one bronze medal.

Andy Gray was denied the opportunity to show the Millwall home crowd the impact he could have on the side when his Den debut was cut short after 55 minutes of the match against Grimsby. By that time Steve Livingstone had scored the only goal of the game for The Mariners to prolong Millwall's poorest home form in several years.

Millwall's season was now teetering like the closing bus scene in The Italian Job. With every home defeat it dangled precariously over the edge, staring the relegation places in the face. Then, with a redeeming away victory, fans started to look optimistically at the slightly smaller gap between them and sixth place - and the chance of escape from what was becoming an increasingly grim latest spell in football's third tier.

With promotion-bound Watford scheduled to end the month with a visit to The Den having suffered defeat just three times all season, it was vital that Millwall steadied the ship with upcoming matches against mid-table Blackpool away and at home to third place Northampton. Those hopes were quickly dashed as a Gray-less Lions were subjected to a Valentine's Day massacre at Blackpool's Bloomfield Road, finding themselves 3-0 behind by the break. Something of a theme was also developing as Blackpool's second goal was scored by yet another Millwall old boy in Chris Malkin.

There was little consolation in the home loss rot being stopped with a goalless draw against promotion hopefuls Northampton at The Den next where the side was bolstered by the return of another old stager in the guise of Rhino Stevens and the general feeling of apathy and grudging acceptance was still in evidence when Champions elect Watford arrived. Barely 7,000 fans saw Shaw score his eleventh goal of the season to give Millwall an unexpected chance to complete a league double over Graham Taylor's side, but normal service was resumed just after the restart when Mooney levelled and the match finished 1-1. The return to the side of Andy Gray helped to ensure that the expected Hornets' onslaught and inevitable winner didn't materialise.

The month petered out with an uninspiring 1-1 draw at Oldham where for once it was the opposition that committed hari kari with an own goal cancelling out Stuart Barlow's opener.

Millwall's league position, in-keeping with their form, had been up and down like the proverbial fiddler's elbow and much of this was down to Bonds being hamstrung by the age old problem of injuries, for which even his most vociferous of West Ham-hating critics must have had at least a scintilla of sympathy. The Northampton match had seen Bonds field his fourth goalkeeper in all competitions that season. Starting with Tim Carter, youngster Nurse had been given a baptism of fire in that home trouncing by Wimbledon after which Nigel Spink took up the gloves, briefly deposed once more by Spink and now Nottingham Forest veteran stopper Mark Crossley was between the Millwall posts. Defence had also seen many permutations which could only have lent itself to the side's inconsistent showings.

Kenny Brown had been an admirable ever-present at right back with the opposite position being shared between Paul Sturgess and Ricky Newman. Now Bonds had settled on Robbie Ryan, an Irish left back who had joined from Huddersfield, who instantly looked at home in the position. The central positions had been ably filled by Brian Law and the returning Alan McLeary with the latter making his 400th Millwall appearance in his second spell at the club.

With McLeary's appearances also hampered by injury as a long season wore on, Bonds no doubt utilised his links with ex-number two Pat Holland at Spurs in bringing in centre back Stuart Nethercott who, like Ryan, seemed to fit straight into The Lions' back four. The irony was that Bonds seemed to be slowly but surely finding the right blend, just as the season was drifting towards its conclusion and had unearthed two players that would play a major part in the club's eventual resurgence.

That was still some way off of course, and on a bleak Wednesday night in Carlisle, it seemed to be further away than ever.

South Bermondsey homestay bites

21

The last hurrah

March 1998...
Paul Gascoigne leaves Rangers to sign for
Division One Middlesbrough; A Fulham fan dies
after being stabbed during crowd trouble outside
Gillingham's Priestfield Stadium after the match
and an Everton fan is prevented from confronting
the referee during their 4-1 home defeat by Aston
Villa.
Liam Gallagher is charged with assault, for
allegedly breaking a fan's nose in Brisbane,
Australia after the fan took photographs;
Millennium Dome construction begins.

They say that the ultimate test of true fan loyalty is to make the arduous trip from the south to Carlisle for a midweek match that has little or nothing at all resting on it. That accolade was well and truly earned by the handful of hardy Millwall souls that stood on the Brunton Park terrace on Tuesday March 3rd 1998 to watch an almost inevitable single goal defeat that did nothing to alter Millwall's league fate, either in terms of the now dead play-off aspirations or draw them any closer to the bottom tier trap door which, despite being unerringly close in terms of position, was still at relatively comfortable arms length.

A much more invigorated crowd at The Den the following

Saturday, perhaps relieved that the pressure of trying to sneak a play-off spot or escape the drop had all but evaporated relaxed a little and almost certainly afforded themselves a wry smile as they watched a single goal by Brian Law derail in-form Gillingham's play-off hopes and complete an unexpected league double of The Gills.

Even better was to follow a week later when, roared on by a boisterous away following at Craven Cottage, Millwall put a spanner in the works of another team's promotion push. When Fulham visited Millwall earlier in the season having just been taken over by Kevin Keegan they were floundering in 17th place but, following that draw, Keegan's side lost just four of their next 20 matches and had made a solid claim for a play-off place. They appeared to be continuing that impressive run when they led 1-0 at the break thanks to a 26th-minute goal from Thorpe, but Bonds' rejuvenated Lions had other ideas and Paul Shaw continued his purple patch with the equaliser shortly after the restart before Andy Gray capped a memorable comeback and rare win at The Cottage for Millwall with a 77th minute winner that sparked wild celebrations in the away end.

A trip to seventh-placed Wrexham gave The Lions the opportunity to be the play-off party pooper for a third match running but the well organised Welsh side were alert to the danger and an early Roberts goal replicated their 1-0 victory at The Den ten games before to complete the double over Bonds' men.

Rock bottom Burnley who appeared to be on their way back into football's bottom division were next to face the demob-happy Lions where a rare Kim Grant goal was enough to settle the twelfth 1-0 match in what was turning out to be a very binary season for Millwall. Once again they were either great or awful, and for as long as they had been promotion contenders, they had now, since Christmas, also been warily looking over their shoulder at the bottom four, before another flurry of unlikely points saw them ready to coast through the final ten games of the season without a care in the world.

Such a relaxed air at a football club in these days of play-offs - and especially so in the third tier where four clubs are relegated - is all too rare, and it often produces an end-of-season run-in of victories or at least unbeaten matches. This wasn't to be the case with Millwall though. Seven of their final eight matches would be against teams in a similar state of flux, with neither play-off ambitions or relegation fears. With thoughts now turning to the World Cup in France, players and fans alike freewheeled through the rest of the season. Even with twelve hours of football still to play, Millwall's was well and truly over and Billy Bonds had overseen his final win as Millwall manager. Preston provided The Den with yet another 1-0 - this time in favour of the visitors - and Chesterfield eased to a 3-1 win in a match that saw a goalscoring Millwall debut for Graeme Tomlinson. The rookie Manchester United striker - who had made the move to Old Trafford after catching their eye scoring six goals in 17 appearances for Bradford - arrived on loan as Bonds once again tried to shuffle his attacking pack, going for youth and lower league over experience. Tomlinson would play just three matches and score that one goal in the briefest of Millwall careers. A week later, Bonds' other striker acquisition would make his first appearance in a Millwall shirt, with a very different outcome.

April 1998
Ian Wright and Paul Gascoigne are added to Glenn Hoddle's extended squad for the World Cup. It is also revealed that he is using faith healer Eileen Drewery to help his preparations for France 98; Nottingham Forest return to the Premier League after rivals Sunderland are beaten by Ipswich.

Mark E. Smith gets into fights and on stage arguments with The Fall bandmates during a gig in Brownies, New York; The Good Friday Agreement, an agreement between the UK and Irish governments, and the main political parties in Northern Ireland is signed.

Millwall's Bristol jinx appeared to be complete when Rovers' striker Lee Zabek scored in the 87th minute to produce what seemed certain to be the fourth consecutive 1-0 result at The Den. So far that season Millwall had been beaten four times by Rovers' rivals City - in both league matches and in FA and AWS cup games. A fifth loss had come in the corresponding league match at Rovers earlier in the season so it seemed only fair to complete the set with a sixth defeat, one which would give them a chance of securing a play-off place. With City already promoted, Millwall fans must have been secretly rooting for Rovers to win the play-offs so they didn't have to play either of the buggers for at least one season.

As was so often the case that season though, Paul Shaw was on hand to score just when Millwall needed it most and his equaliser was greeted by a cheer that was almost as comically ironic as it was joyous.

One event that did slip under the radar that day was the debut of Billy Bonds' other striker signing. Neil Harris had been ushered in as the transfer window was starting to close. Harris had begun his football career at Maldon Town where his goals alerted first Cambridge City and then Liverpool where he had an ultimately unsuccessful trial just four months before Millwall snapped him up. Harris wasn't your traditional footballer, having an established career in the city before Millwall persuaded him to sign and he made his first start for the club just ten days later in that 1-1 draw with Bristol City. He was substituted after 74 minutes and didn't make the squad for the next trip which ended in a 2-0 loss away to Walsall. In the next match at home to Plymouth he replaced goalscorer Danny Hockton with twelve minutes remaining of a 1-1 draw. He was absent from the final two matches of April which both ended in goalless draws away to Wycombe and then Wigan.

If the immediate appearance of a signing from several levels below in the league pyramid seemed like blind faith in Harris' ability by Bonds, it's highly likely that it was quite the opposite. In fact, Bonds wasn't actually keen on signing Harris, a sentiment backed up by his fellow coaching staff. Yet, on the trusted word of well-respected academy coach Mick Beard, they were persuaded to give him a go. Did Bonds throw him in at the deep end in the hope that he would sink and prove him right?

Millwall fans had been made aware of this non-league goal machine that they had successfully pursued and whilst they wouldn't have been expecting instant goals from a player making a step up several levels at a moment's notice, they would have no doubt, given the amount of false dawns they had suffered in recent seasons, assumed that they had seen the first and last of Neil Harris. They couldn't have been more wrong.

The signing of Neil Harris would prove to be a real sliding doors moment in the history of Millwall Football Club and would have an impact on it for the next two decades.

South Bermondsey homesick blues

22

back to basics

May 1998...
Arsenal clinch the Premier League title with
a record ten consecutive victories – after a
Manchester bookmaker had paid out on United
winning the league back in March; Everton survive
relegation on goal difference on the final day of
the season as Bolton are relegated with Barnsley
and Crystal Palace.
Geri Halliwell announces her departure from the
Spice Girls; Nurses Deborah Parry and Lucille
McLauchlan, who had been convicted in Saudi
Arabia for the murder of Yvonne Gilford the
previous year, have their sentences commuted by
the order of King Fahd and are returned to the UK.

Millwall went into their final match of the 1997-98
season in much the same position as they had
12 months earlier. The record books would
show that they occupied the middle of the bottom half of
the Division Two table with a considerable gap between
them and the play-off places but still two wins or so safe
from the drop zone.

It was steady, if unremarkable, but based on the fact
that Millwall fans still had a team to support, could be
considered progress from their position a year earlier.

Fears that 'Agent Bonds' would see their demise to football's basement did not materialise and, were it not for yet more bad luck with injuries, had Bonds been able to field a settled side, that final league position might have been a little healthier. Reality and perspective were once more the order of the day at The Den as fans said their farewells to another instantly forgettable season. Since the move from their beloved old Den, only the inaugural season had seen them maintain any sort of home form and the new place certainly wasn't the fearful fortress that they had enjoyed previously. Millwall fans were certainly suffering a prolonged bout of homesickness since the short move to South Bermondsey.

Millwall Football Club signed off on the 1997-98 season with a somewhat predictable defeat, but at least it wasn't 1-0. An eleventh-minute Witter own goal - which perfectly encapsulated the Lions career of a player who the fans had taken to their hearts despite his flaws and was playing his final game in a Millwall shirt - was cancelled out by a Grant penalty on 25 minutes. Grant had been one of a legion of incumbents with baggage from Millwall rivals that made the season all the more bizarre. With ex-West Ham management and players and cameos from former Palace stars, ex-Charlton man Grant had unwittingly coined a phrase that would be trotted out decades later - somewhat harshly it has to be said.

After arriving on loan from Luton, fans implored the club to sign him following a goalscoring start, only for his goals to dry up the moment he became a full time Millwall player. He wasn't the first and certainly won't be the last footballer to fall victim to such a fate and yet, years later, any player arriving on loan at The Den and getting off to a good start is cast in the character of Kim Grant should he be signed and lose form.

Paphitis meanwhile had endeared himself to fans with

his honest and straight-talking approach. He kept fans informed with regular updates in the matchday programme and didn't patronise or sugar-coat. He signed off in typical fashion, holding his hands up that the season hadn't gone as well as he had hoped, and, quoting the chorus from Chumbawumba's *Tubthumping* which had become something of an anthem for the long-suffering football fan, kept a promise he made when he arrived and bought everyone a drink:

"WE GET KNOCKED DOWN, BUT WE GET UP AGAIN

Finally, as this dismal season ends, have one on me. I said when I came here that if things didn't work out, we'd have a drink and start again. In spite of what has happened this season we still have the same high aspirations as before. So, tear off the voucher in the corner of the back page of this programme and exchange it at one of the bars around the ground for a pint of lager/bitter or a medium soft drink, and let's look forward to better things next season. This offer also applies to our friends from Bournemouth who, like ourselves, have been no strangers to adversity in the recent past. Well done on your Wembley appearance and good luck for next year."

Mark Stein decided the match on the stroke of half time for Bournemouth and five days later Millwall would announce that they had parted company with Billy Bonds after exactly one year in charge. Arriving on May 8th 1997, Bonds left on May 7th 1998 and whilst many Lions fans were openly celebrating the end of Bonds' short reign, which removed the awkward prospect of having to celebrate any success he might bring by having West Ham fans remind them of how they were responsible for it in the same way they had won us the World Cup back in 1966, he left a legacy which wouldn't be truly appreciated for some time. On the Millwall payroll the day Billy Bonds cleared out his desk were the following players:

Robbie Ryan, Stuart Nethercott, Tim Cahill, Steven Reid, Neil Harris, Richard Sadlier, Alan McLeary, Keith Stevens, Marc Bircham and Lucas Neill. All were players that Bonds felt worth retaining in one capacity or another. Cahill and Reid were two 17-year-old youth players given their debuts on that final day against Bournemouth. Neil Harris was once again started and, were it not for injury, Robbie Ryan, Lucas Neill and Stuart Nethercott would doubtless also have made the squad.

Bonds seemed to be on the right track, but Paphitis was not one for letting the grass grow, neither was he too proud to accept that he'd got it wrong and take instant steps to put it right. He knew that in order to bring success to the club, everything had to be just right. He'd undoubtedly misread the room when appointing Bonds, but he could still claim that it hadn't been a complete disaster. An experiment maybe that had both its good points and bad. Bonds' experience had been enough to steady the ship and build a foundation for the next stage. Now Theo Paphitis had learned quickly that the best path to success at Millwall was with Millwall people, and he knew just the ones to do the job.

Within five days of Billy Bonds leaving the club, Millwall announced their new management team: Keith Stevens and Alan Mcleary. Two players with almost 1000 appearances for the club between them, spanning three divisions and experiencing some of the best - and worst - times in the club's history. The club had turned full circle and appeared, mercifully, to have set a familiar course that had worked so well in the past. A culture that both Stevens and McLeary had been a big part of in the 1980s where the club was built around local young talent and anyone arriving from the outside was either a Millwall supporter or Millwall-type player.

Their Millwall mantra from day one was music to every

fan's ears: They would develop a playing style that would be deployed at every level of the club, from junior to youth to first team, enabling players to progress quickly from each level. Whilst it might have been dismissed as simplistic, the level Millwall were competing at demanded a no frills approach.

Football was still, after all, a simple game where only those fine margins at the very top in the Premier League demanded any great level of tinkering or fine tuning. The footballing graveyard is littered with the bones of clubs trying to buy or play their way out. Millwall themselves had seen that approach fail them quite spectacularly just a few years before.

Making a swift return to the club was chief scout Bob Pearson and Academy Coach Kevin O'Callaghan. It was time to go back to basics, back to The Millwall Way. And if Rhino and Macca couldn't pull that off, no-one could.

Nationwide League Division Two Final Table 1997-98

	Team	Pld	W	D	L	GF	GA	GD	Pts
1	**Watford**	46	24	16	6	67	41	+26	88
2	**Bristol City**	46	25	10	11	69	39	+30	85
3	**Grimsby Town**	46	19	15	12	55	37	+18	72
4	Northampton Town	46	18	17	11	52	37	+15	71
5	Bristol Rovers	46	20	10	16	70	64	+6	70
6	Fulham	46	20	10	16	60	43	+17	70
7	Wrexham	46	18	16	12	55	51	+4	70
8	Gillingham	46	19	13	14	52	47	+5	70
9	Bournemouth	46	18	12	16	57	52	+5	66
10	Chesterfield	46	16	17	13	46	44	+2	65
11	Wigan Athletic	46	17	11	18	64	66	−2	62
12	Blackpool	46	17	11	18	59	67	−8	62
13	Oldham Athletic	46	15	16	15	62	54	+8	61
14	Wycombe Wanderers	46	14	18	14	51	53	−2	60
15	Preston North End	46	15	14	17	56	56	0	59
16	York City	46	14	17	15	52	58	−6	59
17	Luton Town	46	14	15	17	60	64	−4	57
18	**MILLWALL**	46	14	13	19	43	54	−11	55
19	Walsall	46	14	12	20	43	52	−9	54
20	Burnley	46	13	13	20	55	65	−10	52
21	**Brentford**	46	11	17	18	50	71	−21	50
22	**Plymouth Argyle**	46	12	13	21	55	70	−15	49
23	**Carlisle United**	46	12	8	26	57	73	−16	44
24	**Southend United**	46	11	10	25	47	79	−32	43

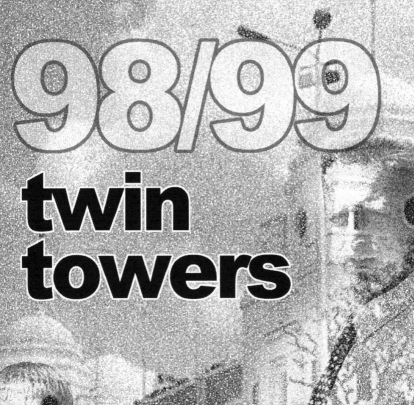

98/99

twin
towers

South Bermondsey homestyle Blues

23

looks familiar...

June 1998...
David Beckham goes from hero to villain at
the France 98 World Cup after being sent off
in England's second round penalties defeat to
Argentina.
The DVD format is released onto the UK market for
the first time...
July 1998...
Manchester United deny reports that they will be
joining a proposed European Super League of up to
32 clubs.
Anti-Social Behaviour Orders (ASBOs) are intro-
duced in the UK following the Royal Assent of the
Crime and Disorder Act.

There was an air of cautious optimism around The
Den as Keith Stevens' side set off for their season
opener at Wigan. Millwall supporters were content
with their new managerial set-up which had a reassuringly
familiar feel about it and as they took to the Springfield
Park pitch, looking resplendent in their new-look bright
yellow away kit reflecting in the late summer sun, it finally
felt like The Lions were beginning their long journey back
once more.

In the previous 30 years Millwall's fate had traced a
similar path. Fallow years followed by a team, usually

made up largely of home grown players, bringing success to the club once more, only for the best players to be sold just as the club were on the cusp of further glory. Millwall never seemed to be able to either get full market value for those star players, or find suitable replacements and so the decline would start again, often punctuated by crowd trouble. Often the disorder would coincide with the teams' success peak, but not always.

Starting this steep upward curve wouldn't be easy. Lions fans who travelled to watch their team's final away match - a Friday night encounter with Wigan - a few months previously will have been party to the club's unveiling of its new owner and investor. Dave Whelan, whose business empire included popular sports retail brand JJB Sports was ploughing unprecedented funds into a club that were currently playing home matches on what amounted to a non-league standard stadium. Audible chuckles could be heard from both home and away fans as Whelan announced brashly to barely 4,000 fans - stood on mud banks, crumbling terracing or sat in the comical little stand - that he intended to see Wigan reach The Premier League with a new stadium fit to host top flight football. In a predominantly rugby town it was a brave boast but one that was unlikely to be taken seriously. Whelan was politely applauded off by the fans who probably felt that two league games with relegated Manchester City that season was probably the closest they'd ever come to 'the big time'.

There was certainly nothing big time about Wigan as Millwall's Paul Shaw picked up where he left off the previous season with a spectacular opener on 16 minutes to give The Lions the lead. Wigan threw everything at them in the second half but Millwall held out to give Stevens a triumphant start to his managerial career.

Another familiar face was on show that day - and another

from the club's glorious recent past. Winger Jimmy Carter had signed from Portsmouth in the summer and his experience and knowledge of the club and fans would surely prove an invaluable. The expected two-legged League Cup first round exit to Division One Birmingham sandwiched Steven's first home league match in charge and brought a second win - 2-1 against Wycombe Wanderers - with goals from Sadlier and a last gasp winner from defender Scott Fitzgerald. Stevens rounded off his first programme notes in typical straight-talking fashion:

"Finally, I'd just like to repeat the message that I've already given to the fans. We're not promising anything at this stage other than honesty and hard work. If you see evidence of that out there then get behind the lads, give them a bit of a boost and let's see what happens."

It wouldn't be long before something very special happened, but for now it was business as usual: expectations raised, and then dashed again, although Millwall did briefly grace the top six, it would be the only time that season.

Nationwide League Division Two - August 22nd 1998						
	P	W	D	L	F	A	PTS
1. Stoke	3	3	0	0	9	4	9
2. Bournemouth	3	3	0	0	7	1	9
3. Fulham	3	3	0	0	5	0	9
4. Walsall	3	2	1	0	3	1	7
5. Colchester	3	2	0	1	5	3	6
6. MILLWALL	**3**	**2**	**0**	**1**	**3**	**4**	**6**

It was just as well Stevens didn't promise anything because August ended with a very familiar look as Millwall tasted defeat for the first time 3-0 away to Bournemouth and ended the month being held at home 0-0 by newly promoted Macclesfield Town in the first ever league meeting between the teams.

September 1998...
Christian Gross is sacked after nine months as
manager of Tottenham Hotspur; Manchester United
accepts a £623.4million takeover bid from BSkyB.
The Union Jack dress worn by the Spice Girl Geri
Halliwell is sold at Sotheby's for £41,320; The Real
IRA announces a ceasefire.

If Millwall fans wanted their Millwall back, there was
certainly evidence of it when they travelled to Burnley for
their next league match. A tame 2-1 defeat where The Lions
were never really in the match showed glimpses of the old
Millwall that were so hard to beat at home, yet struggled
on their travels. Over the years Millwall sides that played
a more direct style seemed to enjoy good home records but
performed poorly away. Conversely, sides that were set up
to play more intricate football often enjoyed a good away
record - but found wins hard to come by in front of their
own fans.

The jury was still out on The New Den of course. Many
still felt that the club had disposed of its greatest asset,
far more valuable than any 20 goal-a-season striker: a
foreboding old ground that no opposition player enjoyed
visiting. Now they had a shiny new stadium which the
likes of Macclesfield and Wycombe - who had recently
been plying their trade in the part time ramshackle venues
of the Vauxhall Conference - loved to visit. The previous
season had seen some impressive away performances,
but some of the worst home form from a Millwall side in
several years, almost certainly depriving them of at least a
tilt at the play-offs. Any success in football has to be built
on being able to win matches on the road as well as at
home, but there's a good reason why the old maxim *"win
your home games, draw your away ones"* almost always
brings success.

Good home form brings with it a more confident
support from the fans who will take a frustrating draw

or unlucky late defeat away from The Den if they feel it can be redeemed at the next home match. From there the momentum builds.

When George Graham took over a Millwall side that couldn't manage a point home or away and were languishing at the bottom of the Third Division in 1982, the first thing he did was stop them conceding goals. It wasn't pretty, but it worked. The next part of the plan was to build a side hard to beat on its own ground and whilst Graham's first full season the following year was one of mid-table mediocrity, sixteen of their 23 home matches were won. On the flipside, they had to wait until late March for their first win away from The Den and only managed two victories on the road all season. The foundation for promotion had been built however and the following season saw that realised with just eight matches lost all season - none at home - and an impressive eight victories away from The Den.

Both Stevens and his assistant Alan McLeary had been youngsters breaking through into that promotion squad and will no doubt have been calling on every bit of Graham's managerial nous from that remarkable spell when the club were saved from the jaws of the Fourth Division and returned to the Second in just two years.

Getting back to winning ways with a 2-0 win over Lincoln was a welcome relief for Lions fans who may have feared the side would revert to its impotent home form of the previous campaign. The match also provided striker Neil Harris with his second start of the season after returning to the side in the previous week's defeat at Turf Moor. It was clear that Stevens was keen to try and establish Harris as his first choice number nine and he repaid that faith in him almost immediately in the next home match. After a desperately unlucky last-minute defeat away to early table-toppers Stoke, Millwall continued to build that fortress at The Den when Harris notched his first goal for the club to spark a second half comeback against Northampton.

The Cobblers had led through a first half Sampson strike but Harris hit the equaliser soon after the restart and the win was sealed by another promising new addition to the side. Tim Cahill, an 18-year-old midfielder who had joined the club from Sydney United FC the previous year belied his even younger looking slight appearance with a tenacity that instantly appealed to Millwall fans. After being carried off in that defeat at Stoke his involvement was in doubt but he showed a typical Aussie grit to put in a box-to-box performance way ahead of his young years.

Whilst Stevens and McLeary's team was starting to take shape, they were still keen to recruit and that led to a bizarre story. Rumours were doing the rounds that Stevens had enquired about the availability of Shrewsbury Town midfielder Lee Steele. Quick to deny the story, Rhino was gobsmacked to be told that Shrewsbury had actually received a phone call from a Keith Stevens asking about Steele. Once it was established that this call had in fact been bogus, it emerged that several similar calls had been made to other clubs, and not just impersonating Stevens. Some called pretending to be Swindon Town boss Steve McMahon. Fortunately this strange spate of calls suddenly stopped, which was just as well as the imposter may well have regretted his prank if both Stevens and McMahon had caught up with him!

Away form continued to provide as much concern and frustration as the home form showed promise, and an early lead at Notts County was quickly cancelled out sending Millwall spinning to a 3-1 defeat to The Magpies ahead of the mouth-watering home league clash with Manchester City.

Joe Royle's City - whose relegation to the third tier for the first time in the club's proud history shocked the footballing world - had not made the blistering start many would have expected and arrived in south London in eighth place. Understandably The Den was rocking and a pulsating first half saw the teams go in at the break goalless. The match exploded into life right at the start of the second period however when Harris sent most of the 12,000 crowd wild with a goal that would prove to be his trademark in the years to come.

Some neat interplay on City's right hand side saw Paul Shaw shield the ball smartly on the edge of the area, knowing that Harris was lurking nearby and ready to pounce. After a few deflections, Harris got the ball under control with his first touch on his left and smashed home in front of The Cold Blow Lane end with his right from twelve yards.

A bad-tempered affair looked to be getting out of control on the hour mark when Paul Shaw and City's Tony Vaughan vied for a lose ball. Vaughan took exception to Shaw's little tug once the ball had gone out of play and a ten-man game of handbags ensued.

Once the dust had settled on the pushing and shoving, referee Messias produced the red card for both of the instigators and a frantic last half hour continued at 10-a-side. But with Millwall missing Shaw keeping the City defence occupied along with Harris, the visitors were able to grab a scrambled last-minute equaliser which they really didn't deserve courtesy of Lee Bradbury.

It had been a steady start in Stevens' and McLeary's first two months in charge. Unbeaten at home with promising signs of progress being made on the pitch. Sadly another old spectre was to return to haunt the club after crowd trouble erupted following the Manchester City match and Lions' chairman Theo Paphitis was having to tackle his first real challenge at the club.

October 1998...
George Graham quits Leeds United after two years
as manager to take over at Tottenham Hotspur; Ron
Reeves, a 55-year-old steward, is killed outside
Highfield Road stadium after being crushed by
the Arsenal team coach just before a game with
Coventry City.
Former Stone Roses singer Ian Brown is jailed
for threatening behaviour towards a stewardess
on a British Airways flight from Paris, a charge
he denied. He is sentenced to four months in
Strangeways Prison, Manchester and is released
after serving two.

Theo Paphitis had until now kept out of the spotlight that
he seemed to enjoy so much the previous season. Whilst
under the Bonds era he was a regular contributor to the
matchday programme, he had seemed to take a step back
this term, perhaps to allow Stevens and McLeary plenty of
elbow room to ease into their jobs.

Events following the Manchester City draw however
dictated that Theo had to make an appeal to supporters via
the programme for the next home match. It was almost a
rite of passage for all Millwall chairmen and Paphitis did it
in his own inimitable style:

*"...Our regular supporters will be well aware that we only
have to sneeze at the wrong time to make the headlines,
and we can't afford anything to happen which will damage
our club..."*

It was a perfectly-pitched piece by Paphitis and a far
cry from the barbed attack by some of the club's previous
incumbents of the Chairman's office when it felt the entire
support was being lambasted and threatened with having
its club closed.

Paphitis stated facts: pitch invasions carried the threat of
fines and ground closures, which would then lead to player
sales to offset the financial implications of that. But he

was also on the side of the vast majority of decent fas who were still unfairly treated by the media. An altogether more sedate 0-0 draw in front of less than half the attendance of the City match saw things settle once more - and Millwall remain undefeated at The Den. All they needed now to turn their solid mid-table start to the season into a genuine play-off push was to start winning away which they hadn't managed since the opening day of the season.

Their next opportunity to do that was at fifth-placed Blackpool. Bloomfield Road had rarely been a happy hunting ground for The Lions but to the disbelief of their travelling fans who had made the trip to the Lancashire coast, an own goal and Paul Shaw strike saw them 2-0 up in 25 minutes. Aldridge pulled one back for The Tangerines just before the break but Shaw was on hand early in the second period to restore the two-goal cushion. Aldridge added his second ten minutes later to leave Millwall clinging on 3-2 for the final half hour but they did so to send them up the table just two points behind Blackpool and within touching distance of the play-off places.

Of course, the real benefit of winning away from home can only truly be redeemed by following that up with three points at home and Millwall's next test of their unbeaten Den record was Kevin Keegan's Fulham.

The west London side had surprisingly missed out on promotion via the play-offs the previous season. Mohammed Al Fayed's investment and Keegan's appointment coming perhaps not soon enough for them to make the leap out of football's third tier at the first attempt. Now in fifth position, Fulham, along with fellow heavyweights Manchester City, were hot favourites to occupy those two automatic promotion places. The others it seemed would have to fight for the play-off scraps.

Another decent Den crowd saw another late goal conceded,

but this time there was no home goal to cheer before it as Kit Symons' 89th-minute goal settled the match, brought to an end Millwall's short-lived unbeaten home record, and left them, more worryingly, with two consecutive blanks in front of their own fans.

Four days later however The Lions were able to redeem themselves with an encouraging 3-1 win at home to York where Harris and Sadlier both returned to the scoresheet and some away resilience was also in evidence with a goalless draw at Wrexham leaving Millwall in seventh place going into the final match of the month at home to Oldham.

The 1-1 draw with the struggling Latics was somewhat typical of how Millwall's season was going and not a million miles away from the Jekyll and Hyde results of the previous campaign. Performances and progress however were a world apart and the fans could see that, even amongst the disappointments, Rhino's young warriors were learning fast.

24

all roads lead to Wembley

November 1998...
Wolverhampton Wanderers sack manager Mark McGhee after three years in charge; Blackburn Rovers lose 2-0 at home to Southampton, leaving them bottom of the Premier League. Manager Roy Hodgson resigns within hours of the defeat.

Walsall's Bescot Stadium is one of the most ideally-placed away grounds for fans to visit. Perched adjacent to the M6 motorway close to the iconic RAC blue glass control centre it's impossible to miss. Millwall fans will probably have been wishing it was located out in the back of beyond and unreachable by humans after witnessing their second comprehensive defeat there in as many visits. It was the first of two trips to early season promotion candidates and the heavy loss at fourth placed Walsall put Millwall's own play-off credentials into stark perspective. Further up the M6, The Lions arrived at Deepdale to play third placed Preston three days later and left a ground where they rarely enjoyed success with a surprise 1-0 win courtesy of a Paul Shaw first half strike. Perhaps those play-off hopes weren't so forlorn after all?

FA Cup involvement ended at the first hurdle for the third

successive season with a 3-0 loss away to Swansea but Neil Harris' growing reputation as a striker continued to blossom when he struck his fourth of the season to give his side the lead at home to Bristol Rovers. Unfortunately The Lions were unable to break their Bristol jinx and a second half equaliser by Jason Roberts made it no wins in seven attempts against the Bristol clubs in the last season and a half of football!

The month petered out with another draw - this time 0-0 away to Colchester but despite remaining off the play-off radar in tenth place, Millwall had quietly put together a useful run of just two league defeats in their last eleven matches. December would start with Welsh opposition in the cup once more - this time at home to Cardiff in the Auto Windscreens Shield, and would herald the beginning of a new chapter in the history of Millwall Football Club.

December 1998...
Brian Kidd steps down as Manchester United assistant manager to succeed Roy Hodgson as manager of Blackburn Rovers; Up to ten Premier League clubs could break away to join a European Super League if the Premier League loses its forthcoming High Court case with the Office of Fair Trading. The case will see the Office of Fair Trading bring a case against the Football League, BSkyB and the BBC in the hope of ending collective bargaining for television deals by Premier League clubs.
Severe gale-force winds hit Ireland, southern Scotland and northern England. Roads, railways and electricity are disrupted.

It's fair to guess that not one of the 1,600 Millwall supporters who bothered to turn up to a cold and frosty Wednesday night Den to see their team face Third Division Cardiff in the first round of the Auto Windscreens Shield could have been contemplating where this particular cup journey would end up.

The truth of the matter is, some of those hardy souls probably only bothered because of the lure of a fixture which had something of a reputation for being a feisty encounter over the years - if not on the pitch then certainly off it. The Lions eased to an unremarkable 2-0 win courtesy of a first half quick fire spell of two in three minutes from Harris and Shaw and almost certainly never gave a thought to the next round which would be a New Year trip to another basement team in Brighton.

Back in league action and Millwall appeared to be flipping the age-old promotion formula of winning at home and drawing away when they drew their third successive league match at The Den with a 1-1 stalemate against Reading and followed it up with another win on the road when goals from Harris and Neill gave them a 2-1 win at Luton.

By now another product of Millwall's youth system had claimed a place in the first team. Steven Reid was a strong, versatile midfielder who now took his place in the centre of The Lions starting eleven alongside Tim Cahill. Both still in their teens, their performances, along with the goals that were flowing with increased regularity from Harris, was further evidence of the progress being made under Stevens and McLeary.

Boxing Day brought another great opportunity for Millwall to get a foothold on those precious play-off places when sixth placed Bournemouth arrived just a point and two places ahead of The Lions. The two teams were equally close in terms of recent form with The Cherries boasting four wins from their last five and Millwall undefeated in their last six. A first half Warren goal for The Cherries was cancelled out by another Neil Harris strike just after half time but a late Stein winner saw Millwall defeated at home for only the second time that season.

The year ended with a 1-1 draw away to another play-off rival and this time it was Millwall's turn to score late when Lucas Neill levelled with eight minutes left at Gillingham.

The year ended on a similar note to the previous one as far as league position was concerned, but the big difference was Millwall's trajectory was very much going in the opposite direction to that late 1997 slump. They may have been back down in mid-table going into the New Year, but just about everything going on at the club was positive - certainly as far as the squad was concerned.

Time was running out if Millwall were going to ensure that the 90s didn't go down in club history as one of its most under-achieving decades. With no promotions won and nothing but play-off failure and shock relegation to show for the last eight years, something memorable *had* to happen in 1999.

25

party like it's 1999...

January 1999...
Nottingham Forest, bottom of the Premier League
and winless for 17 games, sack manager Dave
Bassett after less than two years in charge;
15-year-old Notts County schoolboy forward
Jermaine Pennant signs for Arsenal's academy in a
£2 million deal.
The Euro is launched, but Britain's Labour
government has no plans to introduce the
currency here; Unemployment has fallen to just
over 1,300,000 – the lowest for 20 years; England
manager Glenn Hoddle gives an interview to The
Times newspaper in which he suggests that people
born with disabilities are paying for sins in a
previous life.

If Millwall fans didn't believe the Auto Windscreens
Shield was a genuine chance to see their team at
Wembley for the first time in over fifty years, it was
at least providing some fun target practice. When ex Lions
striker Jamie Moralee gave basement boys Brighton a
fifteen minute lead, it only served to spark them into action
and goals from Harris (2), Lavin, Hockton and Shaw saw
Millwall through to the next round with a comfortable 5-1
victory. The draw for that match would see them play away
to a Bournemouth side who had already beaten The Lions

in both league encounters so far, leaving many of the 800 or so supporters that had travelled to Brighton's temporary Priestfield home to witness that victory assuming it would most probably be the end of their involvement in the competition.

The return to league action at The Den saw a double completed over Wigan thanks to goals from Nethercott, Sadlier and Shaw. Both sides were on the fringes of the play-off race and it wouldn't be the last time they met that season.

Another away victory followed - this time at a resurgent Wycombe Wanderers courtesy of a lone Tim Cahill goal which gave Millwall back to back league wins for the first time since the opening week of the season - also against Wigan and Wycombe.

Once again though, just as Millwall managed to carve themselves out a handy vantage point from which to strike at those top six places with hard earned points on the road, all their hard work was undone with an out-of-character home blip. This time struggling Burnley were able to ease to a 2-1 win at The Den in almost identical fashion to the same result they had achieved at Turf Moor earlier in the season.

After grabbing his first brace for the club in the AWS mauling of Brighton, Neil Harris added a league goal double to his rapidly growing season's tally when Millwall made their first ever league visit to Macclesfield's Moss Rose ground. A routine 2-0 victory put Millwall back on the coat tails of the play-off pack once more and set up the Den clash with sixth-placed Gillingham nicely.

In a Den classic, Tim Cahill's goal on the hour mark cancelled out Nicky Southall's first half opener for The Gills and Harris showed his goalscoring versatility when he gave Millwall the lead eight minutes later and restored that single goal advantage from the penalty spot two minutes after Taylor had made it 2-2. Saunders levelled it again at 3-3 with less than ten minutes left but it was a result - and a performance - that showed Millwall were genuine play-off contenders.

February 1999...
Glenn Hoddle is sacked as England manager two days after his controversial remarks; Manchester United record the highest ever away win in the Premier League by beating Nottingham Forest 8-1. Harold Shipman, the Hyde GP accused of murdering eight female patients is charged with a further seven murders.

Mark Stein had become something of a nemesis for Millwall. The Bournemouth striker had scored in two of The Cherries' last three victories over The Lions and the diminutive hitman quickly made it three out of four when he gave them a fifth-minute lead in the Auto Windscreens Shield third round clash. But Millwall had a goalscoring talisman of their own in the distinctive shape of Paul Shaw. Since joining from Arsenal, Shaw had proved a consistent and reliable goalscorer and had become a great foil for new attack partner Neil Harris. Shaw it was who levelled the tie before half time and the sides could not be separated in either the second half or 30 minutes of extra time, sending the match to a penalty shoot-out. Four of Millwall's five spot-kick takers were successful and it was enough to send Millwall through 4-3 for another date with Gillingham at home in what would be the semi-final of the regionalised competition. That meant The Gills stood between Millwall and a two-legged southern final and a chance to reach Wembley. Suddenly, everyone at Millwall was taking the Auto Windscreens Shield seriously!

Thoughts of Wembley had now understandably taken precedence over what was considered the increasingly unlikely target of a place in the end of season promotion lottery. Millwall's managerial team of Keith Stevens and Alan McLeary, who had been part of the history-making trailblazing Lions team that was the first to appear in the to flight, now had the chance to manage the club to its first post-war Wembley appearance. In fact, only a pedant would actually count that War-time FA Cup final against Chelsea where the teams competing were able to 'borrow' players from other clubs meaning the final line-ups barely resembled the actual clubs they represented.

Minds were certainly elsewhere at Maine Road when Manchester City brushed Millwall aside 3-0 - all of their goals coming in a blistering 15-minute second half spell. With Joe Royle's side now moving through the gears and looking good for at least a tilt at the play-offs, defeat, despite its manner was no great surprise. The 2-0 submission at third-bottom Lincoln a week later though was really cause for concern as Millwall prepared for the visit of The Gills in that eagerly-awaited AWS southern semi-final. Just under 12,000 fans provided an atmosphere worthy of an FA Cup semi-final and if Millwall fans had hoped that Gillingham would be more focussed on their play-off place than a shot at a Wembley final they were soon disappointed as the match was tourniquet-tight from the first whistle. A windswept Den watched a game that ebbed and flowed from end to end like a basketball match as first Reid and then Hesenthaler saw efforts go close for each side. Midway through the first half Harris looked certain to fire The Lions into the lead when he turned smartly and shot inside the area - only to see the ball go agonisingly the wrong side of the post.

Gillingham appeared to gain the upper hand in the second half with Asaba's pace causing the Millwall back four problems and their willingness to shoot from long range almost saw them take the lead when Paul Smith's thirty yard effort was tipped over the bar by Tony Roberts in The Lions' goal. With the Kent side looking certain winners, Millwall rolled their sleeves up and managed to claw themselves back into the game. With the minutes ticking down on normal time and golden goal extra time beckoning, Lucas Neill scuffed a good chance wide of the post following a scramble in the Gills' area and moments later the ball was finally in the net - only for it to be chalked off for a foul on Gillingham 'keeper Bartram.

When Neil Harris found himself in acres of space on the edge of the six yard box as a cross came towards him from the right hand side, Millwall fans prepared to celebrate the inevitable headed winner, only to hold their heads in disbelief as the usually lethal striker saw his effort loop wide. It was to prove the last clear chance of the 90 minutes as the referee blew for full time, sending the match into an extra 30 minutes - which would be decided by the next team to score.

Continuing to attack the Cold Blow Lane End goal, Millwall picked up where they left off and went straight for Gillingham's jugular. Some neat interplay between Harris and Sadlier saw the latter flash the ball agonisingly across the Gills' goal line with no-one on hand to add the final touch and a deep cross from the left was headed out for a corner for Millwall as the pressure piled on. From the resulting Steven Reid set-piece Gillingham appeared to have headed the danger clear, only for Bobby Bowry to loop the ball back into the penalty area where it bounced over the on-rushing Bircham, Harris and their pursuant defenders and fell perfectly into the path of Sadlier who had made a late run from the left where he met the ball perfectly in time with his run to poke it into the roof of the net beyond the desperately flailing Bartram to win the tie and send The Den into raptures.

Millwall were just one step away from Wembley. A two-legged tie against another promotion hopeful who had also got the better of The Lions in league meetings that season - Walsall - stood between them and an unforgettable day out at Wembley in April. League positions and previous results now meant nothing to Stevens' team though. This cup run, which had started as a minor irritant, had galvanised team and supporters in a way not seen since the heady days of the First Division. It was proof that miracles do happen and with hard graft, anything is possible. Of course, they weren't there yet...

Four days later promotion-chasing Stoke visited The Den for a league match which would go down in Millwall folklore alongside that historic golden goal victory. Leading at half time through a Neil Harris goal, Millwall were reduced to ten men after 57 minutes when Reid was dismissed. Undeterred, Millwall extended their lead thanks to Tim Cahill on 65 minutes. To the disbelief of the Den fans, referee Styles wielded his red card once more five minutes later leaving Millwall to defend their 2-0 lead for the final twenty minutes with just nine men.

That they did it so comfortably underlined the steel that Stevens and McLeary had instilled in their team and their eagerness and confidence to continue to blood young talent saw yet another youth prospect make his bow when winger Paul Ifill came on as a sub for Harris. Ifill had been earning rave reviews in Millwall's reserve side and the culture of "If you're good enough, you're old enough" that was now so abundant at the club meant that Stevens had no hesitation in making Ifill a regularly used sub in the next matches.

March 1999...
Former Doncaster Rovers chairman Ken Richardson is sentenced to four years in prison for paying a friend to start a fire at the club's Belle Vue ground in 1995; Tottenham Hotspur end their eight-year wait for a major trophy (and European qualification) thanks to a 1-0 win over Leicester

City in the League Cup final.
Comedian Ernie Wise, who formed one-half of the
Morecambe and Wise comedy double from 1941 to 1984,
dies of a heart attack aged 73 at Wexham, Bucking-
hamshire.

A disappointing 2-1 defeat at Chesterfield was swiftly
followed by a 3-1 home reverse to struggling Notts
County where fatigue and semi-final nerves were clearly
taking their toll on Millwall's increasingly young side.
Remarkably, following on from the previous season's use
of goalkeepers where four different custodians took their
place between the Millwall sticks in 97/99, another stat to
add to the list from that Stoke match saw a debut for young
'keeper Phil Smith who became the fourth to be given the
number 1 jersey that season alongside Nigel Spink, Tony
Roberts and Ben Roberts. It took the tally to seven in
two campaigns when added to messrs Carter, Nurse and
Crossley.

Those two defeats did have a positive impact on Millwall's
preparation for the first leg of the Auto Windscreens Shield
first leg which would be at The Den. With Millwall now
down in tenth place in the table, they could realistically
rule out any hopes of a late surge for a play-off place.
Obviously Stevens and McLeary were far too professional to allow their side to give anything less than 100
percent in every single league game between now and the
end of the season. They would not stop reaching for the
highest possible league position while it was mathematically possible, but with 35 games played and four points
adrift of sixth place, many of the teams in and around the
shake-up had two, three, even four games in hand over The
Lions so expectations would surely have been lowered, if
not publicly.

Unlike the previous two seasons however, there were
no such fears of being sucked into a late relegation fight

with a healthy sixteen point cushion between them and the bottom four. Besides which, apart from the odd blip against Lincoln and Notts County, Millwall were now head and shoulders above the teams in the bottom third of the table both in terms of points and playing power.

All this meant Millwall could now focus solely on beating Walsall over two legs and reaching that Wembley final, with the chance of adding some silverware to The Lions' trophy cabinet and cap an incredible first season for Stevens and McLeary.

That focus was very much in evidence as Millwall gave another boisterous Den crowd the perfect start against Walsall when Tim Cahill gave them a fourth minute lead, but, given the fact that Walsall had scored two and then three without reply past The Lions in their last two trips to The Bescot, there was a tinge of disappointment when referee Eddie Lomas brought the first leg to an end with the tie finely poised at 1-0. Would it be enough? Many thought not.

As is often the way, Walsall were back at The Den four days later for the league encounter and there was evidence of where The Saddlers' priorities lay when a very different version of Ray Graydon's side raced into a 2-0 first half lead. Harris gave the score some respectability at 2-1 but it served notice that if Millwall were going to reach Wembley when the sides met for a third time in seven days, they would have to fight damn hard for it.

The Walsall league match had been designated Millwall's anti-racism focus match. The work of anti-racism campaign group Kick It Out was gaining increasing momentum in the game and, as a club at the heart of a diverse community and one that had strived for many years to promote equality through its various community initiatives, Millwall had launched its own unique campaign and slogan: Lions Have

Pride, Not Prejudice.

Millwall had won just once at Walsall since 1966, but all omens, history and superstition would have been banished from Keith Stevens' dressing room as he sent his side out to make history. Defending such a slender lead put The Lions on a knife edge. They couldn't afford to try and sit back and defend their advantage for a full 90 minutes against such a potent attack as Walsall's, but pushing too hard to extend it left them at risk also.

What they needed was another early goal, and they almost saw their wish granted when Neil Harris broke free on the left hand side of the penalty area only to see his shot skew wide. Millwall continued to throw caution to the wind and use attack as the best form of defence and it was a policy that paid off when Harris found space wide on the Walsall left. His cross was met by Sadlier on the edge of the Walsall six yard box but his first time attempt was blocked, only for the ball to fall kindly for him onto his right foot where he was able to blast it into the top right corner of the net. The expected Walsall onslaught came, but as the home side grew in desperation, gaps appeared for Millwall to exploit and Harris came close to extending the lead when his second half shot hit the bar. As the final minutes ticked by and Millwall's travelling fans edged closer to a final whistle pitch celebration, The Lions continued to push for a killer goal which seemed a certainty when Sadlier released Harris just inside the Walsall box. The striker stormed clear and his dinked shot looked to heading goalwards, only to loop inches over the bar.

As the visiting fans implored the referee to blow for full time, Walsall made another desperate attempt to save the tie, a harmless looking last minute cross and header just inside the Millwall area seemed to have been dealt with and looping towards the grateful arms of Lions' goalkeeper Roberts, only for the stopper to hesitate for a split second, allowing Eyjolfsson to nip in and nod the ball over him and into the net.

With hearts in the mouths of every single Millwall fan at the opposite end of the stadium, another long ball was launched into the Millwall area and somehow fell perfectly into the path of Eyjolfsson, his first touch took him past the outstretched body of 'keeper Roberts, but just as the Walsall fans prepared to celebrate a remarkable comeback the shot was blocked and parried for a corner. With the final minute ticking away a deep corner was swung into the Millwall penalty area and Roberts rushed out to collect, only to flap the ball away to Walsall defender Marsh who lashed a stinging volley goalwards - but mercifully well over.

Roberts' goal kick was the final act and as the ball hung in the air the final whistle sounded sparking wild celebrations from Millwall players and fans alike. As hard as it was to believe, Millwall had made it. They were going to Wembley.

The mandatory topless post-match dressing room celebration images that did the rounds in the local and national press in the following days showed a new, young Millwall side that included Harris, Bircham, Ifill and defender Joe Dolan - yet another academy graduate that Stevens had been happy to throw into the first team under the most pressurised of circumstances. To blood so many young and inexperienced players in a season which was one of the strongest and most competitive in many years at third tier level had paid off handsomely. To have survived would have been an achievement, to thrive as they had done - and crown it with the club's first post-war Wembley final appearance was the stuff of fairytales. Millwall's opponents on that historic occasion would be Wigan who had beaten Wrexham in the Northern area final. Having disposed of three of the division's stronger sides in Bournemouth, Gillingham and Walsall on their way to the final, The Latics, who The Lions had already beaten both home and away in the league, held little fear. Just reaching Wembley wasn't enough, generations of Millwall supporters had lived and died without getting the chance to see their team make that famous walk from the tunnel beneath the Twin Towers. After finally seeing them in the top flight a decade before, this was their holy grail, winning was the only conceivable outcome.

Once again, the energy of cup success saw momentum carried into the next matches with wins at Oldham (1-0) and at home to Wrexham (3-0). Harris took his tally to 17 for the season with another brace against the Welsh side and was on target to become Millwall's first striker since the legendary Teddy Sheringham to score twenty goals in a season. Tim Cahill meanwhile took his tally to seven in all competitions with the winner at Oldham, a remarkable return for a teenage midfielder in his first full season. As they entered April the countdown began until that Sunday on the 18th and the club was soaking up an atmosphere around the place not seen since those heady days after winning the Second Division title back in 1988.

SOUTH BERMONDSEY HOMESICK BLUES

26

Out Of Africa

April 1999...
Manchester United reach their first European
Cup final for 31 years, and only their second of
all time by recording a 4-3 aggregate win over
Juventus.
A bomb explodes in Brixton, South London, and
injures 45 people; A second bomb explosion in Brick
Lane, east London injures 13 people; TV presenter
Jill Dando, 37, dies after being shot on the
doorstep of her Fulham home.

Millwall's preparations for their big day at Wembley
were far from ideal. Talismanic striker Paul Shaw was
battling to recover from injury in time and the injury list
was beginning to lengthen in worrying fashion with young
stars Dolan, Reid, Ifill and Cahill all nursing knocks, such
was the flipside of introducing such raw talent into the
rough and tumble of third tier football.

The biggest blow of such a double-edged sword however
came with the announcement that Millwall would have
to do without the striking services of Richard Sadlier for
the final. Sadlier had been increasingly effective playing
alongside Neil Harris in the absence of Shaw and of course
scored crucial goals in both semi-final and final to get
The Lions to Wembley. The galling thing was, Sadlier's

absence would not be due to injury or fatigue, but as a direct result of that success. He had gained international recognition by the Ireland under-20 squad and had been picked to travel with the squad for the FIFA World Youth Championship that coincided with the AWS final - in Nigeria. Theo Paphitis could not contain his fury at the decision, which was announced in the wake of Millwall's victory celebrations:

"I'm very upset for Richard Sadlier, and angry that he appears certain to be denied the opportunity of enjoying our Wembley day which he has done so much to help us achieve. We did everything in our power to persuade the Irish FA that they didn't need Richard to go to Nigeria for that Under 20 tournament when he is likely to sit on the bench out there. But they are adamant that he must go, and FIFA have made it clear that they will not tolerate any interference from clubs, and will impose hefty sanctions on players and clubs who refuse to co-operate.

I think people who have planned such a tournament at the very time when the season in many countries in a coming to a climax are being irresponsible. The venue is also questionable with political unrest and violence being an additional cause for concern. The English FA have at least stipulated that first team players will not be required to go, but unfortunately the Irish FA, although not their manager Mick McCarthy, have taken a different view, and in my opinion an irresponsible one.

A lad like Richard Sadlier naturally wants to represent his country, but if his country thought anything of him they would recognise that this is probably the last chance he will have of playing at Wembley before it is demolished and would take that into consideration. If he sits on a subs bench in Nigeria whilst his colleagues are gracing the best stage in the world, what is that going to do to him?"

On the pitch, at least one player was able to continue his fine season's form without the distraction of injury or international call-up. A single Neil Harris goal at home to Blackpool was enough to edge him closer to that magic 20 and with 18 goals in all competitions, he would surely be a decisive factor in that Wembley final. The next match would prove to be another bitter sweet blow to Millwall's preparations however. Paul Shaw made his first start in eleven games as The Lions visited relegation-haunted York City and when he fired Millwall into the lead with less than 20 minutes left, it was a huge boost for Stevens and McLeary to seemingly have their potent strike pairing together again with the final just eight days away. That joy lasted less than five minutes though as Shaw was forced out of the match with a dead leg meaning the best he could probably hope for was a place on the Wembley bench.

Things went from bad to worse when York struck twice in the final three minutes to steal the game 2-1 and Stevens didn't hold back in his criticism of what he perceived to be players somewhat understandably protecting themselves from missing Millwall's big day:

"I don't think there was any doubt about it, at York Last Saturday most of our players were thinking only about Wembley this coming weekend, and I must say that as a manager I find it very difficult to accept. As a professional, you should be approaching every game in the same manner, fully committed and desperate to win it. That wasn't the case up at York and I was very disappointed indeed. Other people have suggested to me that with the injury to Lucas and one thing and another it's not surprising that we didn't put in a Millwall performance on Saturday, but I can't find any excuse for people not doing the job we sent them out to do."

Stevens rested almost his entire first choice eleven for the last league match before the final at home to Colchester -

even playing himself for the only time that season. More youngsters were given the chance to taste first team football with Ronnie Bull, Byron Bubb and Leke Odunsi starting.

Kim Grant scored both goals in the opening fifteen minutes of a 2-0 win but the ex-Charlton striker had seemingly fallen out of favour with Millwall's management team since their arrival and the likelihood of him featuring in the final was unlikely. With Shaw unlikely to be able to start and Sadlier scoring the first of the goals for his country in a 4-0 win over Australia that saw them qualify for the knock-out stages, any hopes Stevens may have had that they could fly him home the moment they exited the competition and in time for Sunday's big kick-off were fading fast. But in typical Rhino fashion, he wasn't giving up.

At the same time Millwall were beating Colchester, Sadlier's Ireland were playing hosts Nigeria in a round of sixteen knock-out match. The winners would progress to a quarter final clash with Mali which would be played at the same time as Millwall Auto Windscreens Shield final. Defeat for Ireland left the door open for Sadlier to hot-foot it back to Blighty, but it was only very slightly ajar.

The match kicked off at 4pm local time and Stevens will have probably only had chance to follow the first half at the most before preparing his team. Far from spending the tournament on the bench, Sadlier was leading the Ireland front line and gave them the lead ten minutes before the break making his chances of returning in time for Millwall's big day pretty much dead in the water.

By the time Stevens had debriefed his side after their win over Colchester however, events had taken a turn in Nigeria. The hosts struck a 70th-minute equaliser and after extra time failed to separate the sides, the match went to penalties. Shittu struck the decisive spot kick for Nigeria sending them into the quarter finals and Ireland out.

Sadlier's Wembley dream was back on - but it was going to be tight.

South London was a ghost town on the morning of Sunday April 18th 1999. The initial allocation of 41,000 tickets had been snapped up in no time, and Millwall were delighted when their requested for more was granted. A further 7,000 were sold and Wembley was invaded by almost 50,000 Lions fans, Wigan meanwhile were more modestly represented with the final attendance officially being declared as 55,000. Unfortunately for Millwall, football as we know is decided by the number of goals and not supporters and ultimately The Lions' dream day would end in somewhat typical disappointment.

Stevens was able to name a full-strength starting line-up - but it was only full strength in terms of players whose minds were very much willing but bodies that had weathered a long tough season falling physically just short. Sadlier started but would later admit that he was physically and mentally exhausted by the drama he had played so much more a part in than he expected in Nigeria. So much so that his journey virtually from airport arrivals to Wembley dressing room and on to the huge pitch to play a final was done in an almost unconscious daze.

The carnival atmosphere that preceded with a charity football match and a sea of Millwall flag-waving suggested they had already secured the trophy. This was further underlined when actor Richard Driscoll, a self-confessed Millwall fanatic who was at the time playing vicar Alex Healy in soap Eastenders, couldn't resist saluting the Lions supporters with an impassioned, fist-clenched "COME ON YOU LIONSSSSS" while his celebrity teammates including a bewildered-looking Angus Deayton sheepishly disappeared down the tunnel.

Wigan appeared to be silent by-standers, but as we know,

that is always a dangerous situation in football.

The reality was that whilst Millwall's build-up to the final had been disrupted by injury, international call-ups and erratic results, Wigan's had been anything but. They had been steadily climbing the Division Two table since Millwall had completed the league double over them three months before from mid-table to the edge of the play-off places. If Millwall were hoping that their minds were on those rather than the final, they were to be proven dramatically wrong.

Wigan looked the livelier from the first whistle, with Barlow causing the Millwall defence problems and responsible for the only real chance of note in a low-key first half. It was Wigan doing all the pressing again after the break and Howarth came close to giving them the lead following a quick break after a Millwall attack broke down.

The initial excitement-fed energy quickly sapped from both Millwall fans and players on a warm afternoon and The Lions looked increasingly leg-weary in conditions that are particularly unforgiving on a large expansive Wembley surface. Midway through the second half however, they looked to have found a breakthrough when Harris broke down the Wigan left, a deflection saw him beat the last defender and as The Latics' goalkeeper Roy Carroll rushed out to prevent the Millwall striker form getting a clean shot away, Harris managed to get enough on the ball to edge it goalwards off Carrol's outstretched glove. As Millwall supporters began to celebrate with the ball bobbling slowly towards the line, veteran Wigan defender Colin Greenall silenced their cheers by somehow managing to dive in and toe the ball to safety. It was perhaps another indication of Millwall's season running out of steam that there was no Lions player within 20 yards of the move when they had attacked with such vigour and in great numbers previously. All it would have taken was for Sadlier to be lurking as he had been for that golden goal winner against Gillingham to almost certainly seal victory.

Moments later Millwall survived a penalty shout at the other end when Andy Liddell was sent tumbling by Steven Reid but fortunately what looked a certain spot kick was waved away by referee Wilkes. As the minutes ticked down Wigan seemed to find renewed energy while Millwall seemed to be running on empty. Lions goalkeeper Roberts fumbled a Balmer header from a deep cross yet somehow Wigan were unable to convert the ensuing scramble into a winning goal.

With the last of three minutes added time ticking away, extra time would surely be a bridge too far for Millwall's battle-weary players and Wigan sensed victory. The lively Liddell made another lung-bursting run into the right hand side of the Millwall penalty area and shouts for a handball as he brought the ball under control ready to cross were ignored by the referee. It didn't seem to matter though as his cross posed no threat to the Millwall goal with, for once, no Wigan players in support. Lions 'keeper Roberts left the ball to allow right back Gerard Lavin to deal with it but at an awkward height the Scottish defender was only able to hook it back to direction it came from where Stuart Nethercott had been tracking Liddell. Nethercott then headed the ball out and across the penalty area towards Tim Cahill who had Wigan midfielder Paul Rogers lurking on his left shoulder. With the young Aussie clearly not expecting the ball, Rogers was able to push past him leaving a clear sight of goal and he made no mistake burying the ball in the bottom left corner of the net from twelve yards.

As the small pocket of Wigan fans celebrated, the majority of the stadium stood in silent disbelief. Wigan had won it with virtually the last kick of the match. Even the most partisan of Lions fan would have to admit they probably deserved it on the balance of play over 90 minutes, but to have finally reached Wembley after such a long wait and against an opposition they had already proved they were capable of beating, to not even have the pleasure of celebrating a goal was devastating - but oh so typically Millwall. The Lions' audacious bid to end the 90s with a Wembley win had fallen agonisingly at the final hurdle but the signs for the future and the new century were bright. If any Millwall fan needed a bit of perspective however, they only had to think of Lions fan Remo Lucia. The 51-year-old from Deptford was at Wembley with his son and suffered a fatal heart attack prior to kick-off. A stark reminder once again that it is only a game of football.

There was little surprise three days later when Millwall travelled to a Fulham side that had long since been crowned champions and were soundly beaten 4-1.

The programme for the penultimate match of the season at home to Preston six days after their Wembley dream had died was full of praise for Millwall's support at the Twin Towers, not least from Paphitis:

"YOU WERE MAGNIFICENT!

I want to thank everyone who was at Wembley last Sunday for helping give me one of the biggest buzzes of my life. Apart from the birth of my kids I've never experienced anything quite like it, and although we were all bitterly disappointed by the result, the atmosphere created by the Millwall fans made it a magnificent day nonetheless. The feeling we have now is that we've got some unfinished business and that we've got good reason to look forward to the future. The fact that our fans came out in such numbers is an indication of just what we can achieve with a bit of success here, and we all want it so badly that we won't rest until we see Millwall promoted and get back to Wembley, whether it be this one, or the one they build to replace it. I said after Sunday's game that it's better to have loved and lost than never to have loved at all. We may have lost that Final, and it may have left a bitter taste, but we certainly loved being there in the first place. Another of my favourite sayings is that I do fail, but I succeed more often than I fail. The reason that sometimes I fail is that I'm prepared to try things, and to attempt things that other people say can't be done. This season, we as a football club got to Wembley, against the odds, with a young inexperienced team and with management in their first season in the job. That partially fulfilled one of our dreams, partially! We've got many more dreams.

I'm not going to share them with you right now, it would take forever. But I can assure you that Rhino, Macca and Bob Pearson share those dreams for this club, and along with all the players and staff we are going to be doing our utmost to fulfil some of those dreams for us all.

There was a feeling on Sunday night that we'd let the fans down by not winning that trophy. But all we can do is assure you that we're more determined than ever to give you the success you want and deserve. We thank the hard core of supporters who come week in week out, and the challenge now is to win back some of those who came with us to Wembley. We can promise 100% effort and commitment on our part, and if we fail, it won't be for the lack of trying or determination. You are the Best"

Just to underline how bright Millwall's future was, play-off bound Preston were pegged back by goals from Cahill and Ifill in the last five minutes of a 2-2 draw. Cahill was edging towards a return of ten goals in his first full season and the increasingly impressive Ifill fully deserved his first senior goal for the club. It would prove to be Millwall's last of a season that ended with just that single point to show for the final six matches and a three match losing streak at Bristol Rovers (0-3) and Reading (0-2) and at home to Luton (0-1). But for once, Millwall fans didn't care. The programme for that final match included another 'Free Drink Voucher' on the back which fans could redeem for a pint. Not that they needed it. They were drunk on the relative success of a season that had gone far better than they could ever have hoped twelve months earlier. From the turn of the year Millwall's league position was mediocrity personified, never falling below 11th and never rising above 9th yet it was this steadiness that allowed them to build the team and blood new players without fear of blowing a play-off place or falling into relegation trouble. The fact that there was disappointment in Neil Harris falling two goals short of a twenty goal haul in all competitions showed just how high the bar had now been set.

Wigan on the other hand had taken the momentum of that final win into their last league games and remarkably stole the final play-off place from under Bournemouth's noses on goal average on the final day of the season. With Walsall edging Manchester City out of the top two, Joe Royle's side had to navigate a tricky play-off campaign, first ousting a gutsy Wigan in the semi final and then staging a dramatic late comeback in the final against Gillingham to win promotion at the first attempt on penalties.

The 1999-2000 season would see a much more open Division Two where Millwall would be back even stronger and, for the first time in many years, genuine title contenders.

Nationwide League Division Two Final Table 1998-99

	Team	Pld	W	D	L	GF	GA	GD	Pts
1	Fulham	46	31	8	7	79	32	79	101
2	Walsall	46	26	9	11	63	47	63	87
3	Manchester City	46	22	16	8	69	33	69	82
4	Gillingham	46	22	14	10	75	44	75	80
5	Preston North End	46	22	13	11	78	50	78	79
6	Wigan Athletic	46	22	10	14	75	48	75	76
7	Bournemouth	46	21	13	12	63	41	63	76
8	Stoke City	46	21	6	19	59	63	59	69
9	Chesterfield	46	17	13	16	46	44	46	64
10	MILLWALL	46	17	11	18	52	59	52	62
11	Reading	46	16	13	17	54	63	54	61
12	Luton Town	46	16	10	20	51	60	51	58
13	Bristol Rovers	46	13	17	16	65	56	65	56
14	Blackpool	46	14	14	18	44	54	44	56
15	Burnley	46	13	16	17	54	73	54	55
16	Notts County	46	14	12	20	52	61	52	54
17	Wrexham	46	13	14	19	43	62	43	53
18	Colchester United	46	12	16	18	52	70	52	52
19	Wycombe Wanderers	46	13	12	21	52	58	52	51
20	Oldham Athletic	46	14	9	23	48	66	48	51
21	York City	46	13	11	22	56	80	56	50
22	Northampton Town	46	10	18	18	43	57	43	48
23	Lincoln City	46	13	7	26	42	74	42	46
24	Macclesfield Town	46	11	10	25	43	63	43	43

SOUth Bermondsey homesick Blues

99/00

end of a century

27

White Lions

August 1999...
Arsenal sign Thierry Henry for an estimated fee
of £11 million, reuniting with his former manager
Arsène Wenger; Leeds United sell Jimmy Floyd
Hasselbaink to Atlético Madrid of Spain for £12
million;
A MORI poll shows Labour support at 49%, giving
them a 22-point lead over the Conservatives;
Former Dexys Midnight Runners frontman Kevin
Rowland is bottled offstage at the Reading
Festival, which saw him perform "The Greatest Love
Of All" whilst wearing a white dress;

The 1990s had seen more changes in football than any other decade. Whilst you could point to the game barely changing from the start of the sixties until the end of the seventies, the only significant change seen in the game during the eighties was a depressing decline. The last nine and a half years however had seen the game undergo a complete transformation and was it barely recognisable from the version of the sport that had begun the nineties. English teams were once again competing in Europe and, after a stuttering start, had finally seen success with Manchester United lifting the European Cup in stunning fashion with a last-gasp win against Bayern

Munich to add to their Cup Winners Cup win back in 1991 when the door was reopened to English clubs after a five year absence. The equalising goal in the 2-1 victory over the German giants was scored by Teddy Sheringham. The striker had begun the decade by alerting the top clubs to his goalscoring talents in a 38-goal final season for Millwall which saw him secure a move to Premier League Nottingham Forest. The Clough dynasty was coming to an end there however and after 14 goals in 42 appearances moved on to Tottenham Hotspur where 75 goals in 166 matches was enough to alert Alex Ferguson at Manchester United and he was added to his dominant squad in 1997. After an uncharacteristic slow start, Sheringham soon found his shooting boots once more and was a vital part of United's historic treble-winning team in 1998-99.

Down at The Den, change for the better was in evidence too. There was a renewed feeling of optimism and the joint managerial team of Keith Stevens and Alan McLeary had been able to strengthen their squad with the addition of goalkeeper Tony Warner from Liverpool, defender Sean Dyche from Chesterfield, veteran strikers Paul Moody and Michael Gilkes and midfielder David Livermore. On the way out was Kim Grant who moved to Belgian football.

There wasn't just change in the playing staff either. Keen to try and reinvent the club and its brand, for so long associated with all that was bad in the game, Chairman Theo Paphitis looked to utilise his retail guru status by securing a shirt sponsorship deal with Local Boyz clothing brand Giorgio and hoped for a fresh start with the controversial decision to kit The Lions out in an all white home strip. Whilst the move was popular with fans of a certain age who appreciated the nod to the early seventies days when Benny Fenton's side came so close to promotion to the top flight, some weren't keen to see the traditional blue shirt abandoned and even less so when the new kit's 70s feel was topped off by a return to the club badge of that era. The roaring rampant lion was replaced with the more regal-looking two red lions facing each other. Dissenters on the increasingly busy Internet messageboards such as The House of Fun's Controversial Corner quickly dubbed the badge 'the Pattycake Lions' as online opinion started to compete with the pre and post-match pub chat.

Unconfirmed reports that Paphitis' decision to change the badge was to engender a less aggressive more public-friendly face of Millwall Football Club were quickly ridiculed when The Lions' campaign opened with a 1-1 draw away to newly-promoted Cardiff City.

It was a fixture that was always something of a powder keg affair and this one was no exception, forcing Paphitis to start the season with another statement confirming how much had been done by the club to prevent trouble at Ninian Park. As was so often the case, much of Millwall's intelligence and advice-sharing fell on deaf ears and once again, Paphitis was defending the club and fans instead of condemning them. It went a great deal of the way to keep his relationship with the fans on a good footing, even if some were struggling to come to terms with that new kit and the Pattycake Lions...

Pre-season had been up and down with wins over Welling, Peterborough and Nottingham Forest and defeats to Wimbledon and Crystal Palace. Encouragingly, Tim Cahill, Paul Shaw and Neil Harris were among the goals in those games and it was a 35th-minute Harris penalty that gave The Lions the lead in that opener at Cardiff - only for the Welsh side to level it up from the spot on the stroke of half time. Millwall stayed in Wales for the Worthington Cup first round first leg match at Swansea which ended in a 0-2 defeat so the pressure was on to fulfil that mood of optimism when Wigan visited The Den for the first home match of the season.

Wigan's big project, launched two years earlier by new owner Dave Whelan was now very much in progress. The rickety old Springfield Park ground had been abandoned for the shiny new JJB Stadium which was home to both the town's football and rugby teams and The Latics were now one of the division's big spenders assembling a team that made them one of the early promotion favourites, with Millwall not far behind in the bookies' estimations.

That gap appeared to be a gaping chasm however when Millwall's nemesis Andy Liddell - who Lions fans still insisted handled the ball before setting up The Latics' late Wembley winner four months before - gave them the lead in the last minute of the first half. When Balmer and Barlow struck to make it 3-0 just after the hour mark, the mood at The Den was already darkening. Paul Shaw grabbed what looked to be a mere consolation goal with twelve minutes left but when Tim Cahill made it 3-2 two minutes later, the raucous Den did it's work and roared Millwall onto an unlikely point which was secured, once again from the spot by Neil Harris.

It didn't detract from the fact that Millwall were winless and seemingly leaking goals - underlined a week later in a 3-1 defeat at Stoke. League cup interest ended with a whimper after a 1-1 draw at home to Swansea and a Cahill-inspired lead against the Spireites of Chesterfield was short lived when the visitors snatched a point late on in another disappointing Den display, leaving Millwall ending August winless and in the bottom four:

Nationwide League Division Two - August 28th 1999						
	P	W	D	L	F	A	PTS
21. Blackpool	7	1	2	1	9	15	5
22. MILLWALL	**5**	**0**	**4**	**1**	**6**	**8**	**4**
23. Reading	6	1	1	0	9	14	4
24. Oldham Athletic	6	1	0	0	3	7	3

28

One step forward...

September 1999...
Newcastle United appoint Bobby Robson as their
new manager; Ade Akinbiyi becomes the most
expensive Division Two player when he leaves
Bristol City for Division One promotion hopefuls
Wolverhampton Wanderers;
David Bowie releases Hours, his twenty-first
studio album and the first by a major artist to be
made legally available as an electronic download;

Millwall faced Cambridge at The Den on September 18th still searching for their first league win of the season. The international break for the Euro 2000 qualifiers saw them start the month just a week before with a Tony Warner-inspired goalless draw away to Bristol City giving them their first clean sheet in seven winless matches and the pressure was already increasing on managerial duo Stevens and McLeary.

Not that they were letting it get to them of course. As stalwarts of a Millwall defence for so many years, they knew better than most that no team was relegated or promoted in September and had faith that their new signings would gel and that first win was imminent.

That proved to be the case - but not before a scare. Cambridge took the lead early in the second half and the Butler did it. Martin Butler that is. Just as the Den natives were once again growing restless, Neil Harris restored parity three minutes later and Tim Cahill sealed Millwall's first win with twenty minutes left. It was less than convincing but the sense of relief was palpable.

It was swiftly followed by another - this time 1-0 at home to Colchester - which saw exciting young home-grown winger Paul Ifill grab the goal after being brought on as a substitute for Neil Harris. Finally the climb up the table had begun:

Nationwide League Division Two - September 25th 1999							
	P	W	D	L	F	A	PTS
13. Wrexham	11	4	2	5	15	20	14
14. MILLWALL	**9**	**3**	**4**	**2**	**12**	**12**	**13**
23. Bristol City	10	3	3	4	13	13	12
24. Cardiff City	11	2	5	4	13	16	11

October 1999...
Chelsea thrash Manchester United 5-0 in the first domestic competitive game that United have lost for nearly nine months; 26 players are sent off in Premier League and Football League matches on the same day, the most dismissals on the same day in 111 years of league football in England;
The Ladbroke Grove rail crash claims the lives of 31 people when two trains collide at Ladbroke Grove Junction;
November 1999...
England qualify for the UEFA Euro 2000 football championship with a 2-1 aggregate win over Scotland in the qualifying playoff round; Arsenal announce plans to move to a new 60,000-seat stadium at Ashburton Grove near Highbury - their home since 1913. They hope to be in their new home for the 2003/04 season;
Gary Glitter is jailed for four months for downloading child pornography;

Just as Millwall seemed to be gathering some sort of

momentum though, they seemed to be set right back to square one with a disappointing 2-0 defeat at Gillingham and it was very much the familiar old story that had played out it seemed throughout the frustrating nineties.

A redeeming 3-1 win at Oxford gave The Lions their first success on the road thanks to two goals from Shaw and another from Cahill but the feeling of them taking one step forward and two steps back soon returned when they were unable to back that up with victory at The Den.

Burnley were occupying those top six places that Millwall fans had felt were their realistic target that they had so far fallen so badly short of, and the gap between this Lions side and a shot at the play-offs was clear for all to see as The Clarets took an early lead and looked like dominating the match. With an out-of-sorts Harris on the bench Millwall were starting to rely heavily on the goals of young midfielder Tim Cahill and it was the Aussie sensation that once again saved the day with a point-saving goal with twenty minutes to go. The writing was on the wall however when, three days later, Burnley's fellow Lancastrian promotion hopefuls Preston proved to be far more ruthless with a thoroughly clinical 2-0 win.

It was Millwall's 13th match of the season - with just three of those being won. A league double was completed over strugglers Colchester who had taken a first half lead through McGavin but Paul Moody scored his first goal for the club to equalise before half time and Paul Ifill secured the points with eight minutes left.

It still felt as if the cracks were being papered over however, something that was borne out in a Halloween horror show at Hartlepool which saw The Lions exit the FA Cup at the first round stage for the fourth consecutive season. For a club that once boasted a proud record of cup conquests, the fact that they hadn't managed a win in the competition since the penalty shoot-out success at Stamford Bridge almost five years before was a shocking statistic. Losing 1-0 to the Division Three side underlined just how much work Stevens and McLeary had to do.

That man Cahill was on target again as Millwall started November with a welcome 1-0 win at home to Luton and they finally turned on the style when Neil Harris rediscovered his goalscoring touch in a resounding 4-1 win away to Scunthorpe sharing the goals with Ifill whose pacey wingplay had The Iron buckling every time he had the ball.

Harris seemed to have salvaged a point on the road at Oldham but a last-minute Whitehall goal saw those old frailties return once more and a frustrating 0-0 draw at home to Wrexham had Millwall fans wondering which version of the team would turn up at each game. Three squandered points, just as they had finally broken into the top ten was galling, but things were about to finally take a turn for the better as, almost overnight, everything in Stevens and McLeary's side clicked into place.

First struggling Reading were put to the sword and the strike partnership of Harris and Moody appeared to be a dream pairing. Moody hit his first hat-trick for the club and Harris weighed in with two more as The Lions routed The Royals 5-0. Moody continued where he left off a week later at Blackpool, scoring both in a 2-1 victory which saw Millwall slot themselves nicely into ninth place in the table.

The Lions seemed to finally have that elusive luxury they had been searching for since the days of Sheringham and Cascarino: a prolific strike partnership. Moody and Harris were the classic big man/little man combination. Moody's aerial prowess gave defences nightmares and his ruthless streaked honed over a long career was a perfect foil for the nippy Harris who was now showing similar efficiency in front of goal. As was often the case with the Sheringham and Cascarino duo, if one didn't score, the other one did as was the case next up when Harris hit both in a 2-1 win at Bournemouth. Similarly to Teddy and Cas, if both scored - as Reading learned, you were bang in trouble.

Nationwide League Division Two - November 27th 1999	P	W	D	L	F	A	PTS
7. Stoke City	19	9	6	4	29	17	33
8. MILLWALL	**19**	**9**	**6**	**4**	**30**	**21**	**33**
9. Brentford	19	9	6	4	31	23	33
10. Luton Town	19	8	3	8	23	25	27

South Bermondsey homeless Bijes

28

making history...

December 1999...
Film producer and actor Bill Kenwright completes
a takeover of Everton; Ole Gunnar Solskjaer scores
four goals in Manchester United's 5-1 home league
win over Everton;
Former Beatle George Harrison, 56, suffers stab
wounds after being attacked by an intruder
Alan McGee announces the dissolution of Creation
Records after 16 years...

Millwall's season had suddenly exploded into life. After finding it virtually impossible to break out of the bottom half of the Division Two table though the opening months of the season, they went into December and a home clash with Cardiff just six points adrift of table-topping Wigan.

Two more goals from Harris in front of a healthy crowd of over 9,000 had the game sewn up before the half hour mark and the 2-0 victory catapulted The Lions into the top six. Now there was no excuse for any distractions as Millwall's season was streamlined further still with another cup first round exit. A last-minute Hart goal for Brighton saw The Lions exit the Auto Windscreens Shield at the first hurdle after coming so close to winning the competition towards the end of the previous campaign. Lions fans couldn't have cared less, they were hoping that this season would see them never have to watch their side in the competition for many years. Moody was back amongst the scoring in a 2-1 win away to Wycombe with Ifill getting the other, and Richard Sadlier made a welcome return to the first team by scoring the only goal of the game to see off play-off rivals Notts County at The Den.

In fact after six wins on the spin, Millwall weren't thinking about the play-offs any more, they had the top two automatic places in their sights, with a Boxing Day trip to Bristol Rovers and a home match with Brentford to round off the decade:

Nationwide League Division Two - December 18th 1999						
	P	W	D	L	F	A	PTS
1. Wigan Athletic	21	12	9	0	41	19	45
2. Preston North End	21	13	6	2	36	18	45
3. Bristol Rovers	21	13	5	3	29	13	44
4. MILLWALL	**22**	**12**	**6**	**4**	**35**	**22**	**42**

Defeat at Bristol Rovers to end the run - just as it promised to send them to within touching distance of undefeated leaders Wigan - was somewhat inevitable. A venue where Millwall had rarely enjoyed much luck and a player who always seemed to score against them, Jason Roberts' 85th-minute winner settled the match leaving The Lions to sign off on the decade - and the century - at The Den where the Nationwide League Division Two match between Millwall and Brentford on Tuesday December 28th will be forever lodged in footballing history.

After an unremarkable goalless first half, Gavin Mahon gave The Bees a 49th-minute lead against a worryingly lack lustre Lions but just as Millwall fans were starting to fear their strikers' magic touch had worn off, Harris levelled the match ten minutes later. With a side containing free-scoring midfielders Cahill and Ifill and no less than four on-form strikers, victory was surely inevitable.

Brentford had other ideas however and with Millwall pressing for that winning goal going into the final five minutes, they hit The Lions on the break and appeared to have stolen the points thanks to Martin Rowlands. The familiar sound of plastic seats being slammed back as frustrated home fans headed for the exit was soon replaced with the unmistakable Lions fans' roar as Paul Shaw capped another great performance off the bench by grabbing what looked to be a late, late leveller. But with around seven minutes of added time being played, Millwall sensed there could be more.

And so it came. With the volume cranked up to the max and three sides of The Den demanding one final push, referee Terry Heilbron was studying his watch as the last minute of the match ticked down and Brentford made a final push for a winner of their own. Warner gathered the ball and without hesitation sent out a booming clearance. In his desperation to clear the danger one final time, a Brentford defender could only skim his header under pressure from Steven Reid back to the right side deep in his own half where Shaw was waiting in acres of space. Sensing a dramatic winner, every Millwall supporter to a man who had been on their feet since the equaliser was now on tiptoes, bouncing in anticipation.

Remaining calm, Shaw spotted the approaching Dave Livermore on the opposite side and fed him with perfect pace and precision. Taking the ball in his stride, Livermore blasted the ball into the top left hand corner of the Brentford net sparking absolute pandemonium.

It was Livermore's first goal for Millwall since his £30,000 move from Arsenal. It was also his first senior goal. It was also not only the final goal of Millwall's 1990s, but the last goal scored in any English football in the twentieth century. History had been made.

Nine years previously Millwall had signed off the festive period in a good position for a promotion push in the New Year. They had a strong squad, a midfielder full of goals in Alex Rae and an attack bursting with goals in Teddy Sheringham. Ultimately that first season of the nineties had ended in play-off disappointment. It was to set them off on a journey through the next eight seasons that would see them leave their beloved Den, flirt once more with play-off heartache and see their dream to return to the top-flight dashed once more amid chaotic scenes and a threat to return to the bad old days of hooligan-inflicted punishment.

They had seen a promotion fight fizzle out into a jaw-dropping last day relegation back to the third tier and watch on in continued horror as their club seemed to be heading for financial oblivion and ultimate closure for good.

After being brought back from the brink, John Docherty made an emotional return to the club he had given their finest ever season by leading them to the top flight for the first time in its then 103-year history and helped them avoid slipping into the opposite end of the league for the first time since the sixties.

The awkward association with a legend of one of their bitterest rivals came to a brief end, but history will show that, under Billy Bonds, the foundations for Millwall's revival on the pitch, once Theo Paphitis had secured its future off it, were most definitely laid.

The more familiar and palatable managerial appointment of two of the club's longest-serving home grown players in Keith Stevens and Alan McLeary once again provided that link with those heady Division One days that had ended the previous decade and it was fitting that the pair would deliver another of Millwall fans' long-awaited achievements with their first visit to Wembley since the war.

Slowly but surely things were falling into place. Just had they had done back in 1987. A mixture of exciting home-grown talent and shrewd signings had built a team that Millwall fans loved to watch. Exciting, quick, skilful with a never-say-die spirit and full of goals.

The nineties may have seen Millwall slip back into the third tier berth that the club had occupied for most of its Football League history since joining back in 1920, but a new decade - a new century - promised to bring the good times back to The Den. So much had changed - both for the better and worse - in the years that separated Malcolm Allen's 41st-minute goal that gave Bruce Rioch's Lions the lead at Watford on the opening day of the 1990/91 season until that history-making strike in the final kick of the century on December 28th. Millwall's fans had experienced almost as many ups and down through that relatively short period than most fans experience in a lifetime of supporting their team.

Thankfully, one thing remained the same: Millwall was still the most unique, biggest small club in the world, and they were ready to come roaring back.

South Bermondsey homesick blues

is that it?

So, what happened next?

The 2000s would prove to be just as eventful as the 1990s. Play-off heartache, managerial changes, trouble on and off the pitch and more entries into the club's history books thanks to both individual achievement and team...

Daydreams & Nightmares
Millwall Football Club in the 2000s - part one
By Merv Payne

Coming in 2022...

Also by the author:

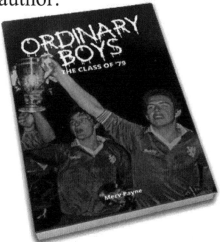

They were just a bunch of ordinary football-mad boys from the local estates, but together on the football pitch they were unstoppable.

This is the story of the Millwall team that won the FA Youth Cup for the first time in the club's history in 1979, but they were so much more than just a team.

An inseparable band of brothers, they defied the odds by not only beating some of the top teams in the country on their way to the final, they out-footballed them.

What was all the more remarkable was that they did it while the football club imploded around them under a constant wave of financial and other off-the-field troubles as it plummeted towards lower league footballing oblivion.

The club's dwindling fortunes would surely be turned around with the help of this new crop of brilliant young players graduating to the team.

Unfortunately, as we know, football isn't always quite as simple as that.

August 1988. The second Summer of Love. The UK wasn't basking in a heatwave, but the euphoric mix of acid house, rave and psychedelia meant that most were completely oblivious to the weather anyway. A year that had started like any other had blossomed in a feel good factor not experienced since the sixties. Love was in the air, house prices were up, unemployment was down and Millwall were in the First Division...

The Lions' appearance at football's top table for the first time in their 103 year history is probably best compared with Punk than Rave culture. Exploding on the scene and sticking two fingers up to the establishment, shocking their way to the top of the pile before being chewed up and spat out and then disappearing as quickly as they had arrived. But this was 1988 not 1976 and while their somewhat unwelcome arrival was no less dramatic and explosive than the opening chords to Anarchy in The UK, there was little bit more class about these boys as they slotted into the high life to the assured but no less revolutionary backing track of Voodoo Ray.

This is the story of a humble south London football club and its unique fans. How a team, built on a shoestring budget and made up largely of locals and boyhood Millwall supporters stunned the football world for a brief but beautiful time back in 1988 when football really was the beautiful game. For two years Millwall rubbed shoulders with the game's elite. Their fans, when they weren't raving in fields or warehouses, were gleefully gatecrashing a party where only the wealthy usually received an invite. There was delight and disappointment, triumph and tragedy, but what a ride.

During the late eighties, the drug of choice was Ecstasy, but for many, just following Millwall was enough, a truly natural high. With contributions from members of that historic Millwall squad as well as fans and opposition players and fans, this is a footballing tale that will never be repeated. Enjoy this trip, and it is a trip...

Signed copies available at:

www.victorpublishing.co.uk/shop

also available in hardback, paperback and Kindle format at:

Also by the author:

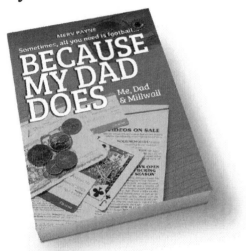

Merv was determined to forge a bond with his dad. It's usually the other way around, but he could tell from a very young age that he'd probably have to do most of the work himself.

After going to their first football match together when he was seven, a shared passion began that would last the rest of their lives - which is just as well, because they had very little else to cement their bond.

Merv's attempts to enhance this relationship through junior football almost had disastrous consequences, but their passion for football – and in particular Millwall – became the glue that held them together.

What Merv really wanted was to share unique, unprecedented success at Millwall with his dad – something that was very thin on the ground in the early eighties. What they both wanted more than anything was to see their team in the First Division for the first time.

Because My Dad Does is a nostalgic journey through the days of the terraces, following your team - with and without your dad - on teletext or the football special, and sharing a once-in-a-lifetime, never-to-be-repeated football season as father and son.

Signed copies available at:

www.victorpublishing.co.uk/shop

also available in hardback, paperback and Kindle format at:

Got a book in you?

PUBLISHING
victorpublishing.co.uk

This book is published by Victor Publishing.

Victor Publishing specialises in getting new and independent writers' work published worldwide in both paperback and Kindle format.

If you have a manuscript for a book of any genre (fiction, non-fiction, autobiographical, biographical or even reference or photographic/ illustrative) and would like more information on how you can get your work published and on sale to the general public, please visit us at:

www.victorpublishing.co.uk

PUBLISHING
victorpublishing.co.uk

Printed in Great Britain
by Amazon